wilderness cookery

complete outdoor meal

y BRADFORD ANGIER

wilderness cookery

C. 1963

8470

STACKPOLE BOOKS

DEDICATION

To my friend and partner

COLONEL TOWNSEND WHELEN

For years the Commanding Officer at Frankford Arsenal—from where in 1804 his great-great-grandfather, Commissary General of the Army Israel Whelen, equipped the Lewis and Clark Expedition—and later the Director of Research and Development at Springfield Armory, Colonel Townsend Whelen, U.S.A. (Ret.), is remembered as Dean of American Outdoor Writers, Dean of American Riflemen, and as the twentieth recipient of the Medal of Honor of the venerable Camp Fire Club of America. This book and its author owe more to him than can be expressed.

BRADFORD ANGIER
Hudson Hope, British Columbia

ACKNOWLEDGMENTS

The author is indebted for some of the illustrations to: David T. Abercrombie Company, Cooperative Extension Service of the University of Alaska, Brion Company, Lodge Manufacturing Company, Randall Made Knives, Sims Stoves, The Ski Hut, The Smilie Company, and the Williams Gun Sight Company.

CONTENTS

CHAPTER 1

SUSTENANCE IN THE SILENT SPACES

When your appetite is sharpened by the healthy sort of outdoor living for which mankind was made, the mealtimes can include some of the best moments of any vacation—if you outfit yourself with foods that keep well, cook readily, and are easy to handle.

Now is not too soon to get started on your provisioning for that next trip back of beyond, for done right it's going to take some time. You'll do best to take foods you personally like and know how to prepare. Experimenting at home and on weekend journeys is the soundest way to find out how much of each item you'll need to round out the sort of satisfying meals you're going to need to keep going under full power.

And they should be satisfying as well as sustaining. As the Hudson's Bay Company says after nearly three centuries in the farthest and most primitive reaches of this continent, "There is usually little object in traveling tough just for the sake of being tough."

Rough it, sure, if you want to prove to yourself the actually very important fact that you can rough it. One day, it's true, anyone at all may be thrown entirely upon his own resources and forced to get along the best he can with a minimum of comforts.

But as far as the preference goes, roughing it is a development stage. Once we've successfully tested our ability to take it, a whole lot of doubts and inhibitions disappear. We find ourself realizing that the real challenge lies in smoothing it. We come to appreciate that making it easy on ourselves takes a lot more experience and ingenuity than bulling it through the tough way.

"Nothing is more important on a camping trip than the

11

grub." As Colonel Townsend Whelen has pointed out, "Most of us go camping to have a good time. If the food is poor, unwholesome, or not what we crave, we have a continual grouch. If it is excellent and there is plenty of it, everything is rosy. Good food even makes up for rain and hard beds. Good fellowship is at its best around good meals.

"Unless you are lucky enough to have a professional cook booked for your party, it will pay you to study the commissary problem in advance. Exercise in the open air doubles the appetite and adds sauce to plain food. In quantity, quality, selection, and in preparation, this food should be good, wholesome, the kind you like, and attractively served."

Far from the humdrum concerns of man-made civilization, it is possible as nowhere else to appreciate the simple pleasures of life—browning frypan bread, steaming coffee, and bacon sputtering over apple-red coals. The crackle of your campfire takes on unexpected coziness, and even the smallest tent all at once seems as snug and satisfying as a mansion.

CHARCOAL GRILLS. Odd thing, wilderness! The instinct for it reaches far into the soul of man, mighty close to the steamy start of things. On this young continent even city dwellers live near their wilderness background, and the campfire remains an integral part of our pioneer heritage, even though it may often find expression today in the charcoal grill. The recipes in this book are adapted for use in the fireplace, backyard, patio, picnic ground, and National Park, as well as in more remote regions.

BASIC GRUBSTAKES. The standard foods taken by experienced outdoorsmen on trips into the farther places of this continent, and which in general form the basis of most grubstakes, include: all-purpose flour, triple-action baking powder, baking soda and a packet of dry yeast if sourdough breadstuffs are to be used, sugar, compact cereals such as quickly cooking rice and oatmeal, corn meal, side bacon which has nearly triple the calories of back bacon, salt pork, oleomargarine, salt, spaghetti and such, powdered milk and eggs, and dehydrated fruits and vegetables. All these are practically free of water.

Some of the more nutritious spreads such as honey, jam, and peanut butter work in well. So does cheese. Practical beverages are concentrated tea powder or tea itself, one of the instant coffees, malted milk, and chocolate. Bouillon solids and dry soup mixes, although short on nourishment, are often welcome because of the easy variety they afford, especially with small game that hasn't had time to age. Seasonings such as powdered celery and onion, pepper, a favorite spice or two, as well as an unseasoned meat tenderizer, may be desirable.

The old Three B days are gone; not that steady diets of beans, bacon, and bannock ever had much glamor in real life after the first couple of days.

THE LIMITING FACTOR. Available transportation will, of course, be the limiting factor in provisioning. A pack horse can balance 120 pounds or so day after day over mountain trails, while a full-size burro can double that. A canoe should not be loaded so deeply that it will have less than five inches of freeboard, depending on the water. This should be increased to at least six inches for windy lakes.

A husky man fresh out of the cement jungles can, without particular difficulty, shoulder about 75 pounds at a stretch over short portages, and he can take his time in making several such trips. He should not usually pack more than 35 pounds, of which 20 pounds may reasonably be food, when hiking day after day for pleasure over high country.

HOW MUCH OF EACH. No one can give you more than an idea of the quantities to take of various items. The tables near the end of the book provide specific and definite information, however, by which you personally can arrive at a reasonable and practical estimate. Detailed grub lists as such are ordinarily of little value, for they seldom suit anyone but the compiler. It all depends on the number of meals you expect to make of each food, how many are to be in the party, and how much of each particular nutriment it will take to make a satisfying portion for each individual concerned.

To determine quantities, you can experiment at home. If you want oatmeal every morning, for example, find out just how much rolled oats are needed to make the breakfast you will likely eat in the woods. Just as a suggestion, take at least double the amount of sugar and sweets you would use at home, for your desire for them in camp will be out of all proportion to what you want in the city.

Here's a yardstick that you may find valuable. Generally speaking, the total weight of reasonably water-free foods you will want to eat should not be less than 2¼ pounds per adult per day. This does not include fresh vegetables and fruits. For purposes of figuring, consult the previously mentioned tables to ascertain the weight relationship of these to their dehydrated equivalents.

All this takes time. But it will pay off in satisfaction, and it's fun.

THE LEAST WITH THE MOST. Fat is, in calories, the most concentrated food. It is also the hardest to come by when living off the wilderness. Butter, oleomargarine, lard, and cooking oils have double and triple the amount of calories that even such a quick energy food as honey contains. If you plan to augment your meals with fish and game, the staples you carry should include a large proportion of edible fats.

Other concentrated foods that have figured conspicuously in rations where space and weight have been stringently restricted include dried shelled nuts, peanut butter, chocolate, dried whole eggs, dried whole milk, and malted milk tablets. If you want a bulky starch, rice is one that cooks up appetizingly with nearly everything.

You can, if weight and space are at extreme premium, use a calorie chart as a basis for figuring how to go about packing the most nourishment with the least trouble. Briefly, you're burning up a certain amount of energy every second. Energy not supplied directly by a sufficiency of food is taken from the body's carbohydrates, fats, and proteins.

Even when you're sleeping relaxed in the most comfortable of eiderdowns, your system is consuming heat units (or calories) at the rate of approximately ten calories a day per pound of body weight. In other words, if you weigh 160 pounds, the least number of calories you'll use each day is 1,600. These basic requirements diminish but slightly, as a matter of fact, even when an individual is starving.

The more you move around and the more energy you expend in keeping warm, the more calories you use. Even lying in your sleeping bag and· reading will increase your basic caloric needs about 25%. The city man who gets very little exercise consumes on the average 50% above his minimum requirements. To maintain his weight, therefore, such a 160-pound individual requires about 2,400 calories daily.

It is reasonable, both from these scientific facts and from personal experience, to generalize that a healthy and fit man enjoying a robust outdoor life can require 20 calories of food a day per pound of body weight—and perhaps more, depending on his activity and on the climate. Cold weather, for example, compels the system to put out more and more heat to keep itself warm. The same 160-pound city man hunting in the north woods can very easily take in 3,200 or 4,000 calories a day, and more, and still trim down lean and hard.

HOW TO PACK. Dry foods such as flour, cereal, beans, salt, and sugar may be packed in small waterproof sacks which are available in a variety of types and sizes from most camp outfitters. You can make them, too. Each should be plainly labeled. Repackage prepared dry foods whenever this can be done advantageously, cutting out and enclosing any special directions. Unless you've plenty of room, foods such as corn flakes should be compressed into as small a space as possible.

Dried meats may be wrapped in wax paper or aluminum foil. Lard, butter, and the like travel well in tightly closed tins such as half-pound and pound tobacco cans. Plastic flasks and bottles made for carrying most liquids are safer and lighter than glass for syrup, oil, and such; but not for most extracts. Powdered eggs and milk will keep better **in**

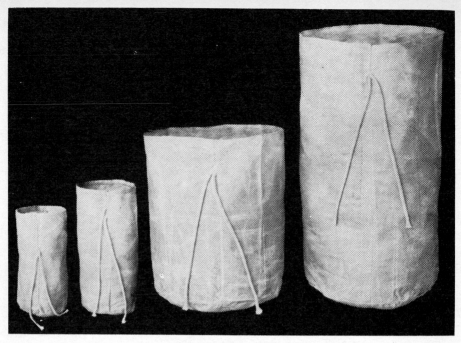

FOOD SACKS.

snugly closed receptacles. Beverages in powder form should also be kept tightly covered. See, also, Chapter 2.

FRESH PERISHABLES. Fabric sacks can be used for carrying oranges, potatoes, onions, and apples when you have room for these. Choose oranges heavy for their size. Thinner, smoother skins usually indicate more juice. If possible, try a few potatoes before outfitting to make sure they're what you want. Pass up any with wastefully deep eyes. Size and color do not affect either onions' flavor or quality. Any with wet necks should be avoided. The very hard, long-keeping varieties are stronger than the Bermuda and Spanish types. With apples, good color usually signifies full flavor.

Cabbage and head lettuce will keep fresh for several weeks if wrapped in waxed paper and then in several layers of ordinary brown paper. Select heads that are heavy for their size. Avoid cabbage with worm holes and lettuce with discoloration or soft rot.

KEEPING COOL. Foods can be kept cool by placing them in a pail that is partly submerged in a shady portion of a brook, lake, or spring. Small amounts of fresh meat will keep for several days this way in hot weather if air is allowed to reach it. Cooked meat, broth, mulligan, greens, and the like will keep better if covered individually. Several yards of inexpensive cheesecloth tucked in the outfit will protect such food when flies become pestiferous.

You can also knock a couple of bottom strips out of a wooden box so that water will circulate through it. Weigh down the bottom of the box with large flat stones and on them place a few perishables. If there is danger from slightly rising water, put these in containers that will safely float. It is usually a good idea to have a partially screened top, which can be held in place by another stone. See the next chapter, too, on this subject.

ABOUT FREEZING. Some of the foods will spoil if allowed to freeze. Days these can be wrapped in bedding. Nights they can be stowed near enough to the reflected warmth of a fire. When traveling with a small outfit and sleeping out in temperatures 60° and more below freezing, I've kept a few canned goods, that otherwise would be burst by the cold, stowed safely out of the way at the foot of my sleeping bag.

When food does freeze, it preferably should not be thawed until it is to be used. Fresh meat and fish keep well frozen. So do cheese and eggs, although their flavors are impaired. The taste and texture of such fruits as oranges are best preserved by letting them defrost in cold water. Frozen potatoes, which take on the aspect of marble, should be dipped in boiling water and their skins scraped off. Then drop them singly into boiling water that is kept bubbling. Cold weather increases a potato's sugar content, so you may find the resulting flavor especially appealing.

CANNED FOODS. Canned goods are usually ruled out except on trips when transportation is of little worry. Otherwise, their weight and bulk can quickly add up to prohibitive proportions. If you cannot expect to procure fresh game or fish, however, you may care to pack along a few of the canned meats. Canned tomatoes always go particularly well in the woods if you can manage them.

Canned butter, although expensive, remains sweet and fresh, but now there is nutritious oleomargarine whose taste for all practical purposes soon becomes practically indistinguishable from butter and which stays good for months at ordinary temperatures.

The most economical way to heat canned vegetables is to puncture the top of the can slightly, as with a small nail, and then to place the container in a deep pan of water. This should not cover the tin, which should be left in the hot water only the brief time necessary to heat the contents thoroughly. It will then give no trouble in opening. Incidentally, if a tenderfoot ever tries to heat that unopened can of soup or beans by dropping it in the campfire, either rake it out in a hurry or stand a long way back.

Nutriment that you may as well capitalize on to the fullest, especially after packing it for miles, is wasted by emptying commercially canned vegetables into a pan for heating. But if you do this, simply warm them before using. Boiling destroys much of their food value.

Don't throw away any of the juice in the can. Containing both vitamins and minerals, it can be profitably used in sauces, gravies, and soups. Seasoned if you want, it also makes a tasty beverage, especially in the bush.

If there are any cans without distinguishing markings except for paper labels and if there is a reasonable chance that your outfit may become wet, scratch the identity of the contents on an end of each tin. I neglected to take this precaution on a month-long river trip in Eastern Canada. We had ample room, no portages, and plenty of hunting and fishing to do in preference to cooking. Therefore, we had an abundance of canned goods, packed loosely in burlap bags so we could trim the canoe more easily. After paddling mostly in rain the first day, and shipping some water in rapids besides, we had to try from then on to pick what we wanted from a perfectly blank array of tins.

The cleanest and safest place to keep the contents of an open can, incidentally, is in that can. Cover this, perhaps with one of several elastic-rimmed little plastic fabrics brought for the purpose, and store away from squirrels and their like in as cool a place as possible. With acid foods such as tomatoes, however, a metallic though harmless taste may insinuate itself because of the acids' eating into the iron of the opened can, so these may as well be shifted to a non-metallic container. Unopened canned goods should preferably be kept at moderate temperatures.

Inspect all cans before buying them for a camping trip. Do this again before opening them. Such commonplaces of wilderness travel as denting, rusting, and freezing all can cause trouble. One test is to press each end of the can. Neither should bulge, nor should it snap back unless the can has been sprung or unless the contents have been frozen sufficiently to exert pressure against the ends although not enough to break the seal. Ordinarily, both ends should either be flat or should curve slightly inward. Seams should be tight and clean with no evidence of any leakage.

When you open a can, watch out for spurting liquid and for any off colors or odors. All are danger signals. Cans should be clean and smooth inside with very little corrosion. If the metal of a meat product can has merely turned dark inside, though, this is only a harmless reaction with the sulphur in the meat.

Whenever there are any signs of spoilage, the wise thing to do is to discard all contents without tasting, burying or burning them to protect wildlife. It's important enough to repeat; do not even touch your tongue to the product. Although you may expel any spoiled food at once, then thoroughly rinse your mouth, that one taste may be sufficient to cause an extremely severe digestive upset if not worse.

Tops should always be well cleaned before any canned foods are opened. For one thing, the metal often picks up poisonous insecticides sprayed in stores. The small roller type of can opener is the easiest to pack and to use. Just stow it, for example, inside the nested cups. The usual attempt to open a can with an ax or hatchet is wasteful at best, while performing the chore with a hunting knife makes cut hands a distinct possibility during and afterward, to say nothing of the damage done a good blade. To avoid metal slivers, begin opening the can beyond the side seam and, unless you need the top all the way off, stop before reaching this seam.

Instead of puncturing the evaporated milk can on top and plugging, taping, or sealing the holes with congealed milk, try making these small openings on opposite sides just below the rim. Then you can close them with a wide elastic band.

SALT. Add cornstarch or a few grains of rice to salt in shakers to keep it dry for easy pouring. A few grains of salt

SALT AND PEPPER SHAKER.

added to cooked foods such as stewed apricots will enhance the sweetening of the sugar content. On the other hand, it is sometimes possible in cooking emergencies to hide the taste of excess salt by adding a small amount of vinegar or sugar. Away from the table, salt is often invaluable as a preservative. The salt draws water from the game or other food to be preserved by the process of osmosis, forming a brine that prevents or retards the growth of microorganisms.

SWEETENING. You can buy one of several so-called sugar substitutes, one tiny pellet of which will sweeten a cup of coffee to the same degree as would a teaspoon of white sugar. Don't do it under ordinary circumstances unless for dietetic reasons. The minute pills furnish the taste, certainly, but they add no fuel to the body.

The various natural sweets such as sugar are among our most readily assimilated energy foods. Granulated white sugar provides roundly 1,750 calories per pound. An equal weight of brown sugar contains 1,670 calories. The same amount of pure maple sugar has 1,580 calories. A pound of honey has 1,400 calories. Good jams average some 1,260 calories per pound, jellies slightly less. For comparison, one pound of fresh lean venison runs about 630 calories. In other words, this isn't the department in which mistakenly to try to save weight.

WILD FOODS. These days you can dine about as easily and well in the wilderness as in the city. Matter of fact, you're likely to find yourself eating considerably better. There may be the drawback of not being able to pick up the numerous frozen specialties featured in modern markets. This disadvantage is more than offset by all the fresh foods that are at hand, free for the taking. Whenever you learn how to recognize and use a reasonable number of these, you're sort of like the old prospector who kneels on a lode of silver while he pans gold and platinum from a creek. Whatever your epicurean whim of the moment may be, you can satisfy it. See Chapter 10 about eating for free.

FATS. Oleomargarine, largely because it keeps so well, is recommended for general camp use. To cut hard margarine or butter cleanly, use a knife that has been heated in hot water.

To protect yourself from popping hot fat, stop the spattering by sprinkling a bit of flour in the frypan. If the grease catches fire, throw a handful of flour on it; either that, or extinguish the flames by covering the burning fat and shutting out the air.

The camp shortening pail can be replenished by pouring in your surplus bacon grease. Excellent lard can also be secured from game fat not eaten along with the lean. Cut this into small bits and melt them down in a pan over low heat. Pour the liquid grease into some handy container, such as a friction-top can, where ordinarily it will harden and become easy to pack. Save the cracklings to eat with lean meat or to munch for lunch some cold noon.

If you are in the fall woods and have bagged a black bear, the pure white grease rendered from the fat of such a trophy is unexcelled for such shortening. If you've collected a grizzly instead, the thick oil rendered from this fat is also excellent. Use it like any other liquid shortening.

THE BEAN FAMILY. Dry beans, peas, and lentils are old-time dehydrated foods that remain favorites in many a vacation camp. See Chapter 8.

JAMS. An outdoor trip is where you really appreciate jams and marmalades. Some campers are bothered by the white crystals that often form in these foods. Looking like mold, such crystals tend to spread through the mixture once the first of them have appeared. Actually, they're the result of sugar combining with the water in the preparation. Although they do nothing for texture and appearance, they are not at all harmful.

YEAST. It is a good idea when using sourdough bread-stuffs to carry a recently dated package of dry yeast in case something happens to the sourdough starter. It's true enough that a fresh starter can be made on the spot by mixing a cup apiece of flour and water in a scalded jar, covering it loosely, and stowing it in a warm place to sour. If the first results are not satisfactory, you can always try again with a new mixture. But the addition of yeast to these sourings will eliminate the guesswork. See details in Chapter 7.

VINEGAR. Here's a pioneer stratagem to stretch supplies of sometimes hard-to-pack vinegar. When half of the vinegar is used, dilute the remainder with an equal amount of water. Then restore its authority by adding a cup of sugar; brown sugar if you have it. The sugar will ferment and supplant the missing acid.

CHEESE. Cheese is one of the most versatile and delectable of camp foods. It may be relished in its natural state or added to everything from soups and salads to sauces to make all sorts of delicious combinations. More than one day I've enjoyed it at breakfast with scrambled eggs, at lunch in a sandwich melted over the noonday tea fire, and at night in a baked macaroni and tomato casserole. Preferences vary. A sharp, aged Cheddar keeps well, as does Edam and Gouda. Provolone is probably the best choice in high temperatures.

If heat makes the cheese rubbery, a solution is to wrap it well and to revive it in a cool stream. If you're going to spend a month or more away from civilization, sew one-week portions snugly in cheesecloth and immerse them in melted wax. You can harmlessly keep mold off cheese to a large extent by wiping the cheese with a clean cloth soaked either in baking soda solution or in vinegar.

MILK. Whether or not you use powdered milk and eggs will depend to a large extent on your preferences and upon where you are. As far as nutrition goes, both compare favorably with the fresh products. Which taste you prefer is mostly a matter of what you're accustomed to; in other words, nothing is the matter with either one, and you can become satisfied with each. A friend of mine, who wrangles dudes up by the brawling Liard River in Northwestern Canada, flew to California the other winter to visit a wealthy sportsman on the latter's dairy ranch. Only thing he couldn't stand was the fresh milk. For years he'd been mixing his with powder and water. Order a glass of milk in many a bustling Far Northern town today, and this is exactly what they set before you.

Powdered milk is especially handy in cold weather if only because the quality of evaporated milk is impaired by freezing, which, as far as that goes, may cause it to spoil entirely by bursting the can. Besides, evaporated milk is still ¾ water. Condensed milk is ¼ water and nearly ½ sugar. Depending on the product, one pound of whole milk powder makes one gallon of liquid whole milk.

Whole milk powder is sometimes a little difficult to mix with water, but there are several ways to get around this. When you open the container, stir the powder and lightly take up the amount you want without packing it down in any way. Even measures are best obtained by leveling off the top of the cup or spoon with the straight edge of a knife. Place the powder on top of the water with which it is to mix. Then stir with a spoon until smooth. The mixing can be speeded somewhat by having the water slightly warm. You can also shake the water and powder together in a tightly closed jar which will subsequently serve as a pitcher.

Better spray dryers have also improved the quality of dehydrated milk. The quick hydrating quality of the newer skim milk powders, however, is the result of a second drying step which gives the particles a porous, spongelike fluffiness that 30 years of research were required to achieve.

Dried skim milk has all the nourishment of fresh skim milk. It has the calcium, phosphorous, iron and other minerals, the B vitamins, natural sugar, and the protein that make liquid skim milk such an important food. Powdered whole milk has all these, plus the fat and Vitamin A found in the cream of whole milk. Adding two teaspoons of butter or margarine to a cup of reconstituted skim milk will make this equal in food value to a cup of whole milk. And it's often a lot easier to mix.

You can even use dried skim milk to make a whipped topping for desserts. Mix ½ cup of the milk powder with ½ cup of preferably ice water. Beat for 3 or 4 minutes until soft peaks form. Then add 2 tablespoons lemon juice, fresh or reconstituted, and beat about the same length of time until it is stiff. Fold in ¼ cup sugar. About 3 cups of topping will result. Serve while you're still ahead.

Containers holding any of the dry milk products should be kept tightly closed, as the powder attracts moisture and becomes lumpy if long exposed to the air. It also picks up odors unless care is taken.

Powdered milk, mixed dry with the flour, makes a valuable addition to biscuits and other breadstuffs. Mornings when you're in a hurry to get away hunting or fishing, milk powder can be mixed directly with cereals such as oatmeal and the breakfast food then cooked as indicated on the package.

Evaporated milk, which is what you may settle for, is homogenized whole milk concentrated to double strength by evaporating part of the water. If you use equal parts of evaporated milk and water, you can utilize evaporated milk as you would any other fluid whole milk. The lumps in evaporated milk are formed by solids settling during storage and are harmless. Cans of evaporated milk can be turned or shaken at frequent intervals during a vacation trip to prevent such lumping.

POWDERED EGGS. An egg is eleven percent waste unless you are going to bake the shells and then pulverize them, as many do to increase the calcium content of their dogs' feed. Seventy-four percent of the remaining yolk and white is water.

Yet dried whole egg has virtually the same food value, includes no waste whatsoever, and is only five percent water. More efficient processing equipment and methods have improved the quality of dried eggs. Varying somewhat with brands, a pound of dessicated eggs is the equivalent of some five dozen fresh eggs. One level tablespoon of the yellow powder, beaten until smoothly blended with two tablespoons of water, again depending on the individual product, equals one hen's egg. And you don't have to bother cushioning those perishable ovals with crumpled newspaper in the more stable types of their own cartons, nor arranging them with the large ends up while camping so as to keep the yolks centered.

The flavor of egg powder cooked by itself is not like that of fresh eggs. Most of us in the United States are accustomed to the latter. Our natural taste reaction, therefore, is that the former is inferior. With different eating habits, as many have witnessed in Europe and elsewhere, this taste prejudice also works the other way around.

In any event, scrambled eggs prepared from the powder come to taste mighty good in the farther places. If you haven't prepared these before, dissolve powdered eggs and milk in lukewarm water to make the proportions of these fresh products you might ordinarily use. Add salt, pepper, and any other seasoning, together with a chunk of butter or oleomargarine. A little flour may be stirred in for thickening. Scrambling all this with ham or bacon gives the dish added flavor.

Never wash whole eggs until you're ready to use them.

However, eggs with clean shells do keep better, so any soiled spots should be wiped off with a damp cloth. Regular washing, though, will remove the natural protective film which aids in keeping out bacteria and odors. Matter of fact, oiling the shells will help the eggs to retain carbon dioxide which, in turn, will serve to retard chemical and physical changes in the albumin and yolk. Such oiling also cuts down moisture losses.

DESSERTS. The dehydrated fruits such as raisins, apricots, apples, prunes, peaches, pears, dates, and figs give everyone plenty of choice. Numerous prepared dessert mixes of one sort or another also afford a wide selection, but find out by experimentation which ones you like before you take to the woods. Especially delicious and nutritious in the wilderness? That dense, heavy fruitcake that ordinarily seems a little too rich for city consumption.

MEAT TENDERIZER. Aging or ripening of meat permits its natural enzymes to become active and to induce tenderness. A number of commercial preparations containing an enzyme are available. The enzyme often used in such tenderizers is papain, obtained from the papaya. You sprinkle the preferably unseasoned variety of enzyme powder over the meat, piercing the meat with a fork to help get the preparation inside. For better results with game, I like to use more than the individual instructions suggest and to let the meat stand a shorter time.

SPICES AND FLAVORINGS. Everybody has his own ideas on these, which is as it should be. Nearly everyone wants a little pepper. Small containers of powdered (not salt) celery, onions, and garlic pack a lot of possibilities. Paprika and powdered parsley combine taste and eye appeal. Then there are nutmeg, cinnamon, and their ilk. Small containers of thyme and rosemary afford occasional taste variations with fowl and red meats respectively. Like the rest, they only cost a few cents and occupy little room. Among the flavorings that seem to taste particularly good in the woods are vanilla, banana, and the peppermint which really touches up chocolate. Then there are lemon and other pure fruit juice powders, crystals, etc. Suit yourself.

CAMP COFFEE. The way I like to make camp coffee is to put a rather coarse grind into fresh cold water, using 2 level tablespoons for every cup of water. Amounts can be varied, of course, for a stronger or weaker brew. Hang or set this over the fire. Watch it carefully. As soon as it boils up once, lift it to a warm sanctuary to take on body for five minutes. Then settle the grounds if you want with a couple of tablespoons of cold water and start pouring.

Unless you have decided preferences to the contrary, though, powdered instant coffee is far preferable to the ground article for general camp use except, perhaps, for those first cups in the morning. It is more economical in weight and bulk, cheaper, better lasting, and both quicker and easier to prepare. It can be made to individual order and without waste.

If you'd like to pocket several pleasant pickups before going on a hike or for a day's fishing, you can ready a number of these in a jiffy beforehand. For each, mix one teaspoon of your favorite instant coffee with an equal amount of sugar. Roll securely in foil. Dissolved pleasantly in the mouth, each will provide the same amount of stimulation and energy as would a similarly based cup of black coffee.

B'ILING THE KITTLE. The northern woodsman, particularly the Canadian, must sip his steaming cup of tea at noon, and contemplate its swiftly seething surface colors, even if he has nothing to eat. This is almost a religion up under the aurora borealis, and it's called "b'iling the kittle." Only a temporary fire is needed, a mere handful of dry wood that will flare up briefly and as quickly fall to ashes, a few feathers of which invariably seem to swirl up to float unheeded in the dark brew. Get the water bubbling. Drop in a roughly measured teaspoon of tea for every cup of water and set immediately from the heat in a safe place. Five minutes of steeping is sufficient.

Tea is something I've long preferred to carry in the usual form, if only for the pleasant rite of tossing a handful of palm-measured leaves into the bubbling kettle. There is powdered tea on the market, however, that mixes immediately with warm water and which tastes a lot closer to regular tea than any of the powdered coffees taste like regularly brewed coffee. This tea can't reasonably be spoiled by improper making, although I suppose some camp cook by trying to make enough for everyone at once can still somehow manage to boil it.

OTHER BEVERAGES. Fruit juices are particular treats in the bush. Lemon, for example, is also sometimes welcome with fresh rainbow trout. A number of consolidated fruit juices are now available, both dried and in concentrated liquid.

Bouillon cubes and powders make hot drinks that taste good around a campfire. A lot of times you'll appreciate them a lot more than you would either tea or coffee. They are also useful for flavoring broths, soups, gravies, and stews. Other worthwhile beverage concentrates include cocoa, malted milk, and chocolate.

CHOCOLATE. Hot chocolate and cocoa in particular have a way of easing those last few steps between fire and bed. As for chocolate bars, these are one of the best known and liked energy foods. It's a common thing on extended camping trips to find a whitish appearance in such chocolate. This does not indicate spoilage, however, but is due to cocoa butter that has separated out. At a temperature no more than 85°, the cocoa butter in ordinary chocolate melts and comes to the surface. It whitens upon hardening. Only the appearance of the chocolate is affected.

INSTANT EVERYTHING. Try the individual dehydrated product first. Do this before you leave home. Then suit yourself. Tastes differ. So do needs. A major error is to load up with dehydrated meals for the entire trip without everyone's doing considerable sampling beforehand. This is especially true when you've little to save but time.

Dehydrated grub is fine in its place. Many of the standards, such as the fruits, are welcome on any table. You can get to like most of the rest, but this often takes weeks and months, far more time than you'll spend on the usual vacation. The vitamins and minerals are there, too, but this is also a secondary factor as far as the average brief fishing, hunting, or camping jaunt is concerned.

Ordinarily, you'll be heading out for fun and relaxation, and the enjoyment of the meals is going to be a determining factor. Unless weight, space, and perhaps temperatures are basic considerations—as in mountain climbing, on extended back-packing hikes away from supply points, and during forced trips into remote regions—dehydrated foods despite their continuing improvements are still most satisfactorily used to supplement, rather than replace, regular victuals.

TRIP TIP. What you take on your camping, hiking, or family fishing trip is pretty much a personal matter. The main thing is not to drive off and leave some wanted item behind. Here are two ways to avoid that disaster.

Unless you live where there's plenty of room, make a check list with a separate column for each group of essentials. One column will be for dry foods, a second for perishables, another for eating materials such as dishes and tableware, and so on.

Tape or glue this list, if that is what you have to settle for, on a heavy piece of cardboard. Use it during preparations, of course, but also have it at hand when you pack for the start. At that decisive moment, recheck items one by one as a preventive measure against going off and forgetting some indispensable.

Those who have ample space can take advantage of the visual technique of building little piles. Place cooking utensils in one group, dining paraphernalia in a second, foods in another, etc. When a certain article is in use at the moment, or needs to be picked up at the store or removed from the refrigerator, a note to that effect weighed down in the proper pile will serve as a handy reminder.

Keep a record for future reference. Note, finally, what is left over at the end of the journey. Such intelligence can guide your efforts when you provision for that next sojourn in the silent spaces.

CHAPTER 2

HEATING AND EATING EQUIPMENT

What remain most fondly in our minds after a wilderness trip are the campfires. The handful of crackling twigs that boils the kettle at noon. The cooking coals at the end of the day's fun, when odors build up in such a way that you can hardly wait for that fresh liver or flaky rainbow. The cheerful flames behind whose sanctuary you sit, while the darkening forest comes to life, and watch moonlit magnificences reserved for those who venture into distant and deserted places.

Then there is that unforgettable first fire at dawn. Because of the air currents set into motion by the blending of day and night, it's colder now than it was during total darkness. The cook maybe deposits an old pine stump, saved for the purpose, in the center of the fading overnight embers. This gives him a blaze like the light of a pressure lantern, and it also helps him to get some warmth into his extended fingers. Pretty soon he's thawed out enough to shove the coffee pot grumpily into the heat. He then begins banging pans around, a little more expressively than necessary. Further sleep soon becomes impossible. The coffee smells too good, anyway, particularly when joined by the aromas of flapjacks and bacon.

Much of the success of a camping trip, as well as a considerable deal of the pleasure, is going to depend on your having the right kinds of cooking fires. This does not mean that campfires, if those are what you use, should be built in just one way. It all depends upon where you are, what you have, and whether your most pressing needs at the moment are for tea, steak, or mouth-tingling barbecue.

THE OPEN FIRE. When conditions are favorable, vacation meals never taste better than when they are prepared

over the red gleaming warmth of wild wood. It is so easy
to regulate the open cooking fire so as to take advantage of
quickly roaring heat, or to provide a ruddy bed of coals
that will break ardently apart for broiling, or to conjure up
such fringe benefits that a dumpling-festooned mulligan will
either simmer or just keep temptingly warm.

When you want to start those food smells tantalizing
your sensibilities in a hurry, the various dry softwoods,
especially when split, will chortle into a quickly flaring blaze.
For steadier and more conservative heat, the hardwoods
are more satisfactory. For an enduring expanse of glowing
coals, you will probably choose when possible such fuels as
oak, hickory, and ash. Or perhaps you'll split up one of the
sweetly black-smoking birches with its inherently hot en-
thusiasm even when green.

Although campfires can be made in numerous ways, the
principles remain the same. An understanding of these
renders fire making under every practical circumstance a
lot more easy. Firewood, for one thing, does not itself actually
burn. A gas driven from the wood by heat is what flames.
To be capable of this, the gas must first combine with the
oxygen in the air.

What we need for a campfire, therefore, is fuel that is
sufficiently flammable to give off combustible gas in sufficient quantity to be lit by the heat we are able to concentrate
on it. This initial fire, in turn, must be hot and lasting
enough to release and ignite more and more gas from
progressively larger fuel.

STARTING THE FIRE. If birch grows in your locality,
the very best kindling is birch bark. Enough small shreds
of this can be pulled off by hand so that seldom will there
be any need, even deep in the woods, to disfigure the tree.

In evergreen country you needn't ever have difficulty in
starting a blaze in any kind of weather. A fairly tight handful of the dead resinous twigs that abound in the lower parts
of all conifers will burst readily into flame at the touch of a
match. The only exception occurs in damp cold weather.
Then freezing moisture sometimes sheathes the forest with
ice. When this happens, the solution still remains simple.

You only have to expose the dry oily interiors of the dead branches.

Shavings from pitch pine light very easily. So do shavings from any dead wood you find adhering to standing evergreens. If no softwood is about, look for dead wood on other trees. If you do have to use fallen litter for kindling, be sure that what you choose is firm and dry.

Fuzzsticks, when you need to bother with them, start a fire quickly. They are made by shaving a piece of wood again and again, not detaching the accumulating curls. These fuzzsticks are commonly employed instead of paper, by the way, to start stove fires in the backwoods. Light fuzzsticks and all other kindling so that the flames will be able to eat upward into the fresh fuel.

Ordinarily, you will use dry materials to get the fire going. The job can also be done with live birch and live white ash, however, by splitting out kindling and making fuzzsticks.

One way to start a campfire, then, is to bunch a few wisps of birch bark on the bare ground. Pile a handful of small, dry evergreen twigs above this. Over this nucleus lean a few larger seasoned conifer stubs. Also in wigwam fashion, so that ample oxygen will reach all parts of the heap, lay up some dead hardwood. Then ignite the birch bark so that the flames will eat into the heart of the pile. Once the fire gets going well, you can shape it anyway you want.

The lighting should almost always be accomplished with a single match. Even on those occasions when plenty of matches are at hand, the thus slowly acquired skill may on some later day mean the difference between a warmly comfortable camp and a chilly and miserably damp one.

The ordinary wooden matches are best. These should be held so that any draft reaching them will feed the fire down the stem where it will be able to keep burning. This you will accomplish in whatever way seems best at the moment. You may face the wind with both hands cupped in front of the flaming match. You may stretch out between the breeze and the carefully heaped flammables so that your body will act as a shield. You may use your jacket or any other handy article, such as a large sheet of bark, to protect the first feeble flames.

There is no time in any wooded area when a campfire cannot thus be built from materials at hand. You can always either find or make a sheltered nook. Even when a cold rain is freezing as it falls, shavings and kindling can be provided with a knife. If you don't have a knife, you can still shatter and splinter enough dead wood with which to kindle a blaze. If, preferably, birch bark is available, one sheet will form a dry base on which to arrange campfire makings, while other sheets angled about and above will keep off moisture until the fire is crackling.

VARIOUS COOKING FIRES. When an experienced camper merely wants to get water boiling in his tea pail and to toast a sandwich or two, he builds a small fire in the easiest way he can, depending on what fuel is nearby. Then he cuts a green pole several feet long. This tea stick he shoves into the ground so that one end extends over the heat. He may adjust its height by propping it up with a rock, chunk of wood, or forked stick. If the ground is hard, he may weigh down the lower end with a billet or stone.

The pail he hangs by its bail at the end of the tea stick. The surface of this stick is generally rough enough so that this handle won't slide; also, branches are usually so trimmed from it that a few projections remain. If necessary, of course, a notch can very easily be cut. Incidentally, a practical tea pail is often only a large tin can with two opposite holes punched near its rim to accommodate a makeshift wire handle.

A larger meal is often prepared with the help of additional angled green poles. However, the round fire is generally not too convenient for cooking purposes. One answer is to arrange a number of such small fires of varying intensities, just as you use different burners on a city range.

But the problem becomes one of most easily supporting the various cooking utensils. As usual, solutions are numerous. One handy method that will do away with a lot of teetering and tipping is to scoop, scrape, or stamp a trench.

This may be about six inches wide and deep and perhaps two feet long. Running this trench in the same direction as the wind will assure a better draft. Get a good fire going in this trench, perhaps by raking it there after it gets blazing well. Then kettle, frypan, and pots can be steadied across it. Such a fire, however, probably won't be successful if either the day is quiet or the fuel is none too ardent.

The answer then may be the more usual above-ground fire but one that's some eight inches wide and four or five feet long. This fire may be contained by two fairly dry logs some four to six inches in diameter, laid either parallel or at a slight angle with the open end toward the wind. If these logs are raised an inch or two by stones or billets, air will be able to circulate advantageously beneath them. Fuel this fire with preferably long split hardwood, and if possible let it burn down either to a hot bed of coals or to a steady blaze which does not flame up more than a foot.

Meanwhile, cut two substantial forked green poles. Drive these upright into the ground at each end of the fire, so that a green crosspiece laid between the crotches will extend the length of the center of the fire. Make pothooks for each kettle by cutting handle-holding notches in forked sticks that can be inverted over this crosspiece. Or carry several pothooks made by bending short lengths of coat-hanger wire into "S" shapes.

A convenient variation of this technique is to use two green poles on either side of the fire instead of the somewhat seasoned logs. Take pains to raise these evenly above the ground, perhaps notching the supporting billets if that's what you're using. Such green poles will take a long time to burn through. Just set your cooking utensils across them.

GRATES AND IRONS. A substantial wire grid, available from dealers in camp equipment, will provide a convenient base on which to set pots and pans above a wood fire and over which to broil meat. Some of these have folding legs which, stuck into the forest floor, will hold kettles and frying pan above the heat.

My own experience, however, has been that these sharp extremities can be somewhat of a menace when one is on the move. I have removed them, also partly to save weight. The grids can as handily be laid across rocks or billets. In a stony and often in a treacherously soft spot, this has to be done anyway.

A similar arrangement, less bulky to pack, is two .iron rods about one-half inch in diameter and four feet long, or flat or angle irons of similar stiffness. Support them above

CAMPFIRE GRILL.

your fire with rocks or logs at each end, and have them just far enough apart so the smallest kettle will not slip down between. If transportation is no problem, a sheet of metal to lay across these will give you much of the convenience of a stove.

SMOKE. Ever notice how smoke seems to follow you around a campfire? Matter of fact, it actually does follow you. Reason for this is that smoke is pulled into the partial vacuum made by any nearby object. The antidote? Create a larger attraction than that of your person. One way to go about this is by building the fire against a boulder or sandy bank. Or locate some other bulk or surface nearby, always a safe distance from the heat.

SAFETY. It does not pay to take chances with a fire. Never kindle one on surfaces made up largely of decomposed and living vegetation. Fire will sometimes eat deep into such footing. An individual may think he has put it out. Unseen and unsuspected, it may smolder for days and weeks. It may lie nearly dormant during an entire winter. With the warmth and increasing dryness of spring, it may regain new vigor until one hot day a strong wind may cause it to erupt into a growling, exploding, devastating forest fire.

When you leave a camp or bivouac in a potentially dangerous area for more than a few minutes, put out that fire. Saturate it with water. Stir up the ground beneath and around it, working and soaking ashes and dust into mud. Dig around it until you are certain no root or humus will lead the blaze away like a fuse. Feel with your hands to make sure that all heat has been safely diminished. Examine the vicinity for any activity resulting from sparks and flying embers.

Particular precaution must be taken in some country when a dutch oven is used underground. In a few areas, especially during the dry seasons, this shallow kettle with its rimmed cover should not be so used at all except when you remain on the spot. Make sure in any event wherever fire can be a menace that the oven is buried in mineral soil and that no combustible material of any sort, be it roots or decaying forest litter, is near enough to be started smoldering.

CAMP STOVES. In spite of all that can be said for an open fire, there are times when a stove either is necessary or is at least indicated by common sense.

The most popular camp stove today is one that uses gasoline for fuel under its one, two, or three burners. In many cases the gasoline stove solves the cooking problem admirably, especially when it comes to boiling and frying. A separate oven can be used for baking.

This type of stove is ideal and often a must for many public camping grounds. It is good for the places where firewood is no longer to be had and where space may be limited. It is excellent for those automobile tourists who like to cook their own meals beside the road, both for the

GASOLINE CAMP STOVE.

pleasure of eating outdoors and because of the very real economies thus afforded.

Such a cooking fire can be lighted immediately. The even and easily regulated heat will allow the refugee from the city range to put out good meals with a minimum of effort and guesswork. Such a stove is fine, too, for travelers in those areas where nonresidents are prohibited from lighting an open fire except when accompanied by a resident or a licensed guide.

Gasoline stoves are inexpensive, easily and compactly packed, and durable. They can be used if desired atop a handy metal stand that supports them at normal stove height and, when not in use, folds into a small bundle that is easily stowed in the car or boat.

TINIEST STOVES. The one-burner primus stove is often the answer for winter sports enthusiasts, fishermen and mountaineers who climb beyond the tree line, and even motorists who like to heat water or cook very small meals inside their cars. These light, efficient little heaters may be obtained in units burning alcohol, kerosene, gasoline, canned gas, and similar compact fuels. For example, there is a 2½-pound combination selling for about $15 which includes: one 3½-pint casserole, one 2½-pint casserole, one

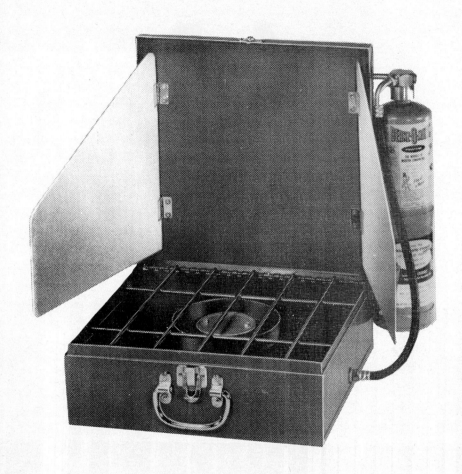

PORTABLE PROPANE GAS COOK STOVE.

lid pan, one upper and lower wind guard, a pot holder, a strap, and a gasoline stove, all nesting into a space 8¼ inches in diameter and 4¾ inches high. Lightweight, leak-proof aluminum fuel bottles are also inexpensively available. The big, catalog-issuing camp equipment dealers stock a functional variety of these units and combinations.

WOOD-BURNING STOVES. Whenever a stove is to be

used where firewood is available, a sheet-metal model burning this fuel has decided advantages. You'll seldom see one today in city stores, and they're unfamiliar to campers with little experience. But along the receding frontiers in whose forests you still encounter old-timers, these wood-burning models usually are the only portable stoves ever considered.

PRIMUS COOKING COMBINATION.

Such a stove usually weighs a little more than the gasoline stove. Although available in folding types, it is generally bulkier. But there is no fuel to transport, and the sheet-metal stove is not difficult to carry even over a portage or on a pack horse.

You can cook on it in the rain. With a little care, it will safely warm closed tents. Many sourdoughs, as a matter of fact, have no other stove, not even in their home cabins. It is easy to dry clothing around it. Broiling and toasting over an open pot hole can be a comparative pleasure.

It is particularly handy for river trips in the large outboard motor boats that travel the broad and often sluggish streams at the roof of this continent. There, odds and ends

SIMS FOLDING STOVE WITH SHELF, OVEN, AND TANK.

of driftwood quickly afford concentrated heat, protected from the ravenous winds often howling along such shores. By providing a shallow box filled with sand, you can even cook afloat.

If the stove you select has an oven, baking and roasting will be possible. If it is without an oven, a folding reflector baker or a separate collapsible oven can be used.

COLLAPSIBLE OVEN.

CARBON MONOXIDE. Be sure there is plenty of ventilation when you have any sort of a stove going in any enclosed area including a tent. Carbon monoxide is more of a threat to outdoorsmen than is generally realized. It is a colorless gas. It has no odor. Being cumulative, it often so weakens a victim that by the time he is aware that something is wrong, he no longer has the strength to do anything about it. There is not even any prior difficulty with breathing to warn him. Carbon monoxide is a potential danger in any closed area where cooking or heating is going on. The best precaution? Good ventilation. You'd think that a tent, certainly, would therefore be a safe place. But when, for example, tent fabrics have been closed by waterproofing in some instances and by frost or rain in others, small stoves going overnight have sometimes killed all occupants.

DUTCH OVEN. Here is the one and only. It's not that this old-fashioned oven of cast iron doesn't have its disadvantages. It's awkward and heavy to carry unless you're traveling by pack train, boat, or car. Furthermore, although it holds the heat, it will rust if not kept well greased. Other varieties, such as those made of aluminum, are both lighter and easier to keep clean. But they're for city stoves if anywhere. They wouldn't even come close to getting the job done over outdoor fires.

What you want for food in the farther places is a heavy, thick, cast-iron pot with a similarly rugged top, lipped to hold a ruddy bed of coals. If your dealer doesn't have one, write the Lodge Manufacturing Company in South Pittsburg, Tennessee. The model I find most satisfactory for my own use with small parties is 12 inches in diameter, 4 inches deep, and 17 pounds in weight. Models are also available 8, 10, 14, and 16 inches in diameter.

The dutch oven you get should have squat legs both to keep the bottom safely above the otherwise scorching ardor of hot embers and to anchor the contraption levelly. It will also need a convenient handle by which the hot top can be lifted and a likewise easily manipulated bail by which the entire contrivance can be moved. Both of these jobs can be performed with the help of a forked stick cut on the spot. When I'm shifting the coal-heaped lid, though, I help balance it with a second stick held in the other hand. You'll also need a shovel. One of the husky, folding models available at surplus stores is convenient to carry. Dutch ovens are used both above and below ground, as detailed in the chapter on breads.

Old-timers season their dutch ovens, when they first buy them, by boiling grease in them. Otherwise, they'll tell you, the cast iron which is porous will give trouble in making food stick. This is a sound precaution when you buy those heavy iron frypans, too.

REFLECTOR BAKER. The way to add a really luxurious touch to meals cooked over open fires is to bring along a

REFLECTOR BAKER.

reflector baker. Described at length in Chapter 7, one of these holdovers from pioneer years can also be effectively utilized with ovenless stoves and with the most modern charcoal grills. Dealers sell reflector bakers in sizes to fit your needs.

Some hints? Because these contrivances roast and bake with reflected as well as direct heat, you'll get better camp-fire results if the warmth from your open blaze is directed toward the opening by some reflecting surface such as a rock or a high back log. Two ways to keep this oven from cooking too fast on the bottom are to place the oven several inches lower than the fire or to base the blaze on a slow-burning green wood so that its concentration of heat will be a bit higher than the lower part of the oven. You need flames for this sort of cooking; not coals. The reflector baker may be set as close as 8 inches to the leaping blaze.

GRIDDLE. A griddle will clear the way for the quick serving of bacon, eggs, and flapjacks in quantity. One of

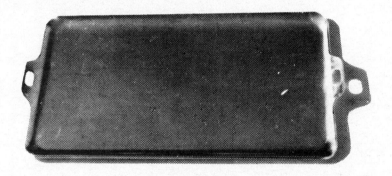

GRIDDLE.

these plates can be laid across a couple of logs between which a cooking fire has largely burned to coals. Matter of fact, such a griddle can also be used as a substitute stove top to keep cooking utensils steady and free of soot. Magnesium griddles are the lightest available. Unless you plan to wrap them in papers, it's a good idea to make or buy a protective traveling cover so as to keep the rest of the outfit clean.

FOIL. Aluminum foil cookery is the modern version of enclosing food for cooking by bundling it in moist leaves, clay, or dripping green seaweed. This modern method also encourages food to retain its juices and to warm evenly. Therein, as a matter of fact, lie the shortcomings. Meat wrapped in foil, for example, is steamed rather than roasted or broiled. The deliciously crisp brownness is missing. There are ways around, of course. But these largely erase the virtues of simplicity.

A fish can be roasted directly on the coals if it is first wrapped in oiled foil, and in the case of small catches you can impart a certain charred touch by toasting it unwrapped beforehand on a forked stick. With large fish, you can help along the taste by cooking sliced tomatoes, diced onions, bacon, chopped peppers, and the like in the foil along with the fish.

Then there are the vegetables and such whose taste this variety of cooking does not seriously impair. The major drawback to any large amount of foil cookery, from the vacationist's viewpoint, is that its nature is more that of an occasional novelty. It does not really lend itself to serious cookery. Once in a while it's fun. But in the long run you save no time or energy. Most importantly for go-light campers on extended trips, you also save no weight. This is not to say that aluminum foil does not have innumerable admirable outdoor uses. Many of these are considered elsewhere.

NESTED COOKING UTENSILS. You'll need cooking and eating paraphernalia. Pots, pans, dishes, and tableware from home will often do.

For the lone camper, the practical minimum is two small kettles with covers and with bails by which they can be hung over a fire, a frypan with preferably a folding handle, a table spoon and usually a light fork, and a cool cup. The frypan will serve as a plate; the cup as a bowl. One's pocket or sheath knife can be used whenever necessary.

Two nesting aluminum kettles, the larger holding about 1½ quarts, together with an 8-inch frypan with conveniently folding handle, are available from dealers in camping goods. Weighing less than two pounds, they add no appreciable bulk to a pack, inasmuch as food and other essentials can be packed within them. Even when there are two or three people in the party, this same outfit can suffice; along with a plate, cup, spoon, and fork for each individual.

Best of all for camping is a small nested cooking and eating kit made of a light, tough aluminum compound. Anyone who has ever burned himself on aluminum, however, will agree that the nested cups, and preferably the plates as well,

NESTED COOKING OUTFIT.

ONE-MAN NESTED OUTFIT.

may well be of stainless steel. The frypan, too, should be stainless steel. I bought an outfit of this sort when I first started going into the real wilderness, and I've used it without replacement or changes ever since. Matter of fact, many of the components are so handy that even when I'm in the city one or another of them is still used almost daily. How-

FOUR-MAN OUTFIT.

ever, some flimsy and highly impractical sets are on the market. Buy your nested outfit, if you get one, from the best established and most reliable sporting goods dealer you can get in touch with. Cost is surprisingly low.

Light fabric holders available for the pots and frypan permit their being cleanly packed, when camp is moved frequently, without a whole lot of work scouring off the black every time. Actually, a certain amount of this exterior blackness makes for faster and more even cooking. You can also secure fabric knife, fork, and spoon rolls that, when you set up camp, can be handily hung to a tree or tent.

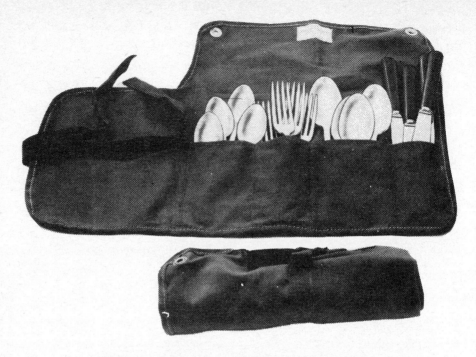

KNIFE, FORK, AND SPOON HOLDER.

When you get home, spots and discolorations on aluminum ware can be removed by using a solution made by dissolving a tablespoon of cream of tartar in a pint of water.

A durable set of nested aluminum measuring spoons takes up very little space and can be handy in both the kitchen and eating areas. If you don't take a regular measuring cup, mark accurate proportions plainly on one of your drinking cups.

MIXING SURFACE. Simplest and handiest thing to take along for mixing and working purposes is a thin sheet of plastic. This can be easily washed, quickly refolded, and conveniently carried from one vacation spot to another with a minimum of bother.

Matter of fact, one of the most convenient things for each individual to carry when picnicking, camping, hiking, skiing, fishing, hunting, or otherwise vacationing outdoors is a thin sheet of lightweight plastic, perhaps five feet by seven feet. This will quickly fold into bandanna handkerchief size, small enough for the pocket of a sport shirt. It can be drawn over the head and shoulders as a protection against wind and rain, laid atop the lower boughs of a tree as a shelter from a storm, spread on the ground as a picnic cloth, and used as a clean waterproof wrapping for a deer liver or a string of sleek bright trout.

AXES. The ax is an almost indispensable tool for the woodsman, many of whom rate it even above matches as the most valuable item to have along in the bush. The full sized ax is not really needed in the average warm weather camp, however. That with a 2½- or perhaps a 3-pound head is big enough for most vacationists.

The handiest ax for packing outside an automobile, although not for any great amount of work, is the Hudson Bay model with a narrow butt and a face of normal width. This model, because of the narrow poll through which the handle is attached, does not hold up too well for heavy work. But for ordinary camping requirements, where weight is a consideration and you still want an ax, a Hudson Bay with a 1½-pound head and a 24-inch handle will do a lot of jobs. A metal-riveted leather sheath should ordinarily be added. The Hudson Bay ax, incidentally, is a convenient one to tie to your saddle.

If you are going to be using a vacation ax very much, you will probably be most satisfied with an ordinary single-bit model with about a 2½-pound head. A handle or helve about 26 to 28 inches long is generally enough, though some may find they can swing the longer 36-inch handle more naturally and therefore more safely. In any event, if you adopt one length handle and use it exclusively, you will come to do better and safer work.

AXMANSHIP. The main thing is to be careful. You can ruin a hunting or fishing trip mighty easily with just one stroke that lands a fraction of an inch from where you want it to go. The best general precaution is to anticipate the worst and to be so placed that even if it does occur no one will be hurt. A sharp ax is safer than a dull one in that it is not so prone to bounce off the wood.

Be prepared to have the ax glance off a knot and have

your feet and legs where they will not be hit. Take the time to clear away any shrubs or branches that might catch the blade. Don't take the risk of steadying a billet with hand or foot.

Avoid, too, the common practice of leaning a stick against a log and half-chopping and half-breaking it in two. A lot of head injuries from flying wood have resulted from that all too prevalent habit. When you're felling a dead tree for firewood, watch out that another tree doesn't break off the top and send it crashing back toward you. In other words, there are a great many possible misadventures. The more of these you can foresee and guard against, the less will be the possibility of an injury.

When you stop to think of it, axes are far less dangerous than such a common substance as glass. Shortcomings do not lie in the ax, but rather in the individual. Use the ax with a nice easy swing. Don't hurry your back stroke. Then let the gravity fall of the ax do most of the work, and you'll be able to cut for extended periods without pressing. Bring your eye to the exact spot where you want the edge to strike, and practice until it does always strike there. Give a slight twist to the blade at the very end of the stroke.

SAWS. It is usually much easier and faster for campers to saw wood than to chop it. If you are using a wood-

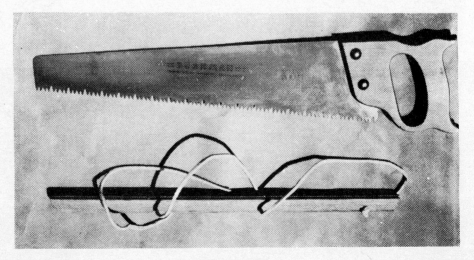

CAMP SAW.

burning stove, such a tool will be invaluable for working available fuel into the right lengths to fit the firebox. Even when you're bivouacking in weather nippy enough to argue the companionship of an overnight blaze, a saw will make the task of accumulating enough fodder for that campfire a comparatively easy one.

The long slender blade of the Swede is a favorite. It is so thin that it speeds through logs with a minimum of effort. It is so light that it can be handled easily in any position. The long narrow blade is so flexible that, except during extreme cold, it can be coiled to the circumference of a saucer, held together by a cord wound and tied among its teeth, and wrapped with a piece of canvas for carrying. The two-piece, light, tubular handle is easily slid apart and packed.

HATCHET. The light hand ax with about a 12-inch

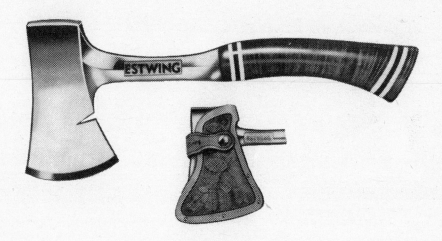

HATCHET.

handle will do all the work necessary in many summer or auto camps and on backpacking trails. The average camper will use it with more effectiveness and greater safety than he will a long-handled ax. Such a hand ax can be useful when you're butchering, although you'll have to touch up the blade afterward. A neat way for even a novice to go through a heavy bone is to hold the hatchet in place, rather than trying to swing it, and to drive it by hammering on the back. This tool also works well enough in procuring wood for a small cooking fire. Secure a substantial sheath for it, but don't ordinarily carry it on your belt. Most of the time this is both inconvenient and uncomfortable. Stow it instead in a rucksack or in a game or saddle pocket.

MEAT SAW. A lot of hunters carry only hatchets or,

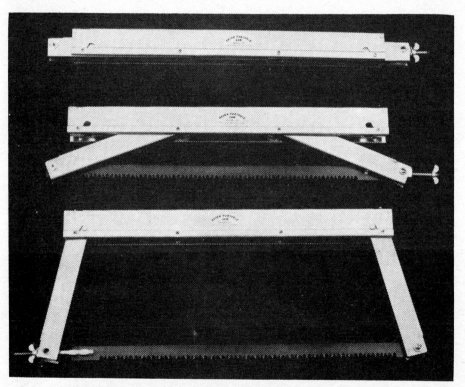

FOLDING SAW WITH BOTH MEAT AND
WOOD BLADES.

if they're traveling by canoe or cayuse, axes. I also like a meat saw, small enough to stow in my packsack. Besides other uses, such a saw is the only conservative way to cut up frozen portions.

COOK'S KNIFE. You need a knife constantly afield, and for many purposes. For example, the camp cook will require one for slicing bread and meat, paring vegetables, and for a dozen other chores. Any fair-sized knife will do for such duties. Unless you're traveling particularly light, however, it is better to have a special one for kitchen work. This blade is almost sure to get such rough treatment that it would take a lot of work to keep it sharp enough for other jobs. Aside from that, a kitchen knife both performs better and holds up more satisfactorily if not given the fine edge desirable for pocket and sporting knives.

COOK'S KNIFE.

One reason for this is that meat is carved and bread sliced more easily with what is actually a sawing action. A coarse edge made by sweeping the blade forward a few times against a carborundum diagonally from heel to tip, first on one side and then on the other, actually resembles saw teeth. This most functional edge can be quickly renewed by the same process.

A small butcher knife, particularly one of those stocked by specialists in outdoor equipment, goes well with most outfits. Have a sheath for it, and keep it in the bundle with the knives, forks, and spoons. Do not oil and thus soften this leather. Not only does the knife then become difficult to encase, but the point has a tendency to catch and puncture the flexible and often curling leather. Saddle soap the sheath instead, or use ordinary shoe polish on it.

CLEANING CARBORUNDUM. Carborundums are used so often in camp that it's little wonder that these abrasive stones become more and more clotted with grime, thus progressively losing their effectiveness. To restore the cutting ability of your dirt-clogged carborundum, just put the stone in a good bed of coals until it is red hot. Then it will be all right again.

COOLER. For fixed camps where refrigeration is a problem, capillary attraction may be harnessed to help solve food-keeping difficulties. Start by building a wooden frame in the general size and shape of an orange crate. Make one side a hinged door. Put in several shelves of slats or poultry wire, making them as open as possible so as to encourage circulation. Then screen the box to assure its being fly proof.

Tack burlap over the contraption, lapping this generously at the door and leaving the top and bottom folds both long and loose. Place a large pan of water on the top of this food container. Immerse the top burlap ends in the water. Capillarity will keep the burlap saturated. If the box is set or suspended in a breezy spot, evaporation will do the cooling.

PAILS. Plenty of water is wanted at most campsites, and sources of supply are often some distance away. Collapsible and folding canvas or rubberized buckets are procurable and are handy for certain kinds of camping. For other types of vacationing, such as automobile camping, two galvanized pails will be cleaner and more convenient. Breakables can be packed in them during traveling.

PACKING FOOD. Available inexpensively from a number of outdoor outfitters, small plastic bags are excellent for packaging all dry home mixes suggested in this book. These bags can be readily sealed by a hot iron. If you want to reuse them, close them instead with one of the adhesive cellulose tapes.

Lightweight unbreakable plastic bottles and flasks of a wide variety of styles and shapes are on the market. You can get these to carry cooking oil and other inert liquids. The storing of whisky and liquors in polyethylene is safe for periods of up to two and three months.

Both regular and high density polyethylene containers are suitable for use with vanilla extracts. However, they have not proved satisfactory with other extracts because aldehydes and esters in these cause a softening of the polyethylene. Such extracts, therefore, are better left in their original glass containers which may be wrapped in tape for safety.

Although high density polyethylenes have been found suitable for use with spices, the essential oils present in significant quantities in black pepper, nutmeg, mace, etc. attack regular density containers of this sort.

In the case of motor campers in particular, regular packages and bottles can be carried without much difficulty if some semblance of order is maintained. A couple of minor hints? If the glass-top jar you take from home sticks, instead of risking injury by prying, just pull the jar rubber far enough out of position to release the seal. If you have to make a cork smaller, cut a small wedge out of the center so that the edges will fit closely.

Paraffined fabric food bags are light, sanitary, moisture-proof, and inexpensive. They impart no odor to the food, and they pack compactly. A good way to label them is with tags or wax crayons. When you transfer a packaged food such as a dessert mix to one of these bags, it's a sound idea to cut out and include the printed instructions. You can also get substantial cotton bags and stow a number of these in a large waterproof sack for protection. Strong, durable plastic bags with tie cords at the top leave contents visible from the outside, but during really rough going they must be protected from abrasion and puncturing.

CHAPTER 3

PREPARING GAME AND FISH

GAME ANIMALS

How good would the choicest corn-fed beef taste if the steer were shot four times through the paunch and chased several miles? Suppose the rancher hacked into the entrails while butchering it, letting additional juices and waste matter mingle with hair in the meat. He might then leave the unskinned carcass lying a couple of days, with the sun working on one side, the damp ground on the other, and flies all over. Eventually, suppose he hauled the beef over the sweltering hood of his car and jolted it through dust, heat, and fumes for a few hundred miles before flopping it down for the locker man to skin, section, and refrigerate. That's the way more than one deer is mishandled, and if the prime steers got the same treatment there'd be as much conversation about "gamy" beef as there is about "gamy" venison. When people honestly and open-mindedly react this way to wild meat, the odds are that the animal was not dressed out properly and that, in addition, the meat wasn't cared for afterwards as it should have been. There is no good reason for any of this.

IS THROAT CUTTING NECESSARY? When you shoot a large animal, it serves no useful purpose whatsoever to run in and cut its throat with the motive of bleeding it. A modern bullet so disrupts the chest or abdominal cavities that they fill with blood almost immediately. No more than a few spoonfuls of blood will be released by this kind of sticking.

But the animal should be gutted as soon as possible. Then turn the body belly down and drain out all the blood. If you're going to use the skin, try not to spill blood on it, as this is difficult to remove. When the animal has been cleaned out, take fistfuls of grass, moss, or leaves and wipe the chest and abdominal walls clean and free of moisture. The blood itself acts as a good solvent in doing this. Get the inside walls as clean and dry as you can. Never use water.

BUTCHERING. When you come to your kill, don't try to hang up the animal unless this can be quickly and easily accomplished. Ordinarily, the job is apt to be difficult and unreasonably time consuming. If this is the case, it will be sufficient to have the carcass with the head uphill and the rest of the body slanting downwards. If even that is not possible, try to get the animal's chest up on a rock or log.

Turn the animal belly up, propping it in that position with rocks, logs, stakes, or whatever else may be handy. Or a line between a hind leg and a tree will hold it. Then make a very short center cut at the lower end of the breastbone just below the lowest ribs. As soon as the knife slits through skin, fat, and meat into the body cavity, insert the first two fingers of whichever is your master hand into the opening.

KNIFE.

Hold the entrails down and away so that the knife will not penetrate them. Then extend the incision down to the rectum, circumventing the active external milk glands if any and then returning to lift and cut away these easily disengaged tissues. Cut around each side of the major sexual organ and around the rectum, taking care not to puncture either. The contents can quickly taint the best meat unless any areas of contact are trimmed away. Carefully free the ducts leading to each. Preferably, tie them off with a piece of string or lace so that nothing will escape from them.

Then with your sleeves rolled up and wrist watch removed, reach up into the upper end of the abdominal cavity and cut the diaphragm loose all around. This is the membrane that separates the organs of the chest from those in the abdomen. Now reach with your secondary hand into the top part of the chest. Find and pull down on the windpipe, gullet, and large arteries. Cut them off as close to the neck as you can. This is one operation where, because of the close and obscure quarters, you have to take particular care not to slash yourself.

Now the entire contents of the chest and abdomen are free except for occasional adhesions along the backbone. These can be quickly torn loose by hand. You can now turn the animal on its side and dump out the viscera. As you work down towards the stern, take care to poke the two tied ends free so they will fall out with the remainder. It is then that you wipe the inside of the animal as dry as possible, after dragging it away from the discards.

DELICACIES. Save the heart, cutting this free from the little pouch of membrane in which it is lodged. Be sure to lay the liver beside it on some clean area such as a piece of bark, a rock, or a patch of snow. Secure the two kidneys as well. All are delicious. You may also care to save the white sheets of abdominal fat which will render into excellent lard for cooking. Unless you are going to have the head mounted, slit the underneath of the jaw deeply enough so that you can pull the tongue down through this opening and sever it near the base. A blood-proof bag is handy for carrying these back to camp.

COOLING. What you do next will depend to a large extent on circumstances such as weather, weight, and terrain. You may be able to hang the game by the head. You will at least be able to turn it so that the body opening can be propped open with sticks in order that the meat will cool as soon as possible.

Covering the carcass with a mass of well-leaved boughs will protect the flesh to a large extent from the shifting sun, as well as from birds which may be already waiting for a chance to whittle away at the fat.

If blowflies are bad, you should either have enough cheesecloth to cover the cavity or a cheesecloth bag in which the entire animal can be placed. Bluebottles and other winged pests will still probably get at it to some extent. When these have been particularly thick, I've found it effective to douse the underneath few of a mass of evergreen boughs with one of the effective and unobjectionable personal fly dopes such as Pellent, taking care of course to keep this off the meat. You can examine all openings and exposed spots when you pack the animal out, in any event, and wipe or cut away any eggs and larvae.

If rain is threatening, a better procedure is to turn the animal so that it is draped, back uppermost, over a rock or log. The body cavity must be freely ventilated in any event. Turning a freshly butchered deer on its belly in the snow, for example, will cause the meat to start to putrify noticeably even overnight in temperatures well below zero.

PACKING. The easiest way to get the venison out of the woods is usually with a horse. This is a common practice in the West. In the East, some hunting camps keep a horse for this purpose. If the animal is spooky, stroke and pet it some and during the process rub a little of the blood on its nose.

Ordinarily, you can tie a deer across or in front of the riding saddle. With something such as a moose, you'll perhaps cut it up and divide the sections between two animals. If snow is on the ground, you may drag a large unskinned quarry by its head after cutting off the legs.

Dragging is most easily accomplished with a harness. However, you can take a half hitch high around the tail, bend back the hair, and then take a second half hitch around the now doubled tail. The usual saddle horse will then skid out even a good sized moose or elk without any lasting discomfort if conditions are halfway favorable. If the experience is a new one, the horse will probably settle down better if you remain in the saddle as much as possible.

Snugging the rope around the saddle horn is not such a good idea.

MANPOWER. Deer can be dragged headfirst by a couple of husky hunters. They are often carried on a stout pole, back hanging down and feet tied up over the timber. The head should also be lashed up so that it won't dangle and continue to throw the load off balance. As a matter of fact, a deer lugged more than a short distance in this fashion will swing so much that you will very probably soon be weighing the advisability of cutting a second pole and using the two of them as a stretcher. This, once the animal has been tied on solidly, can be borne at any height.

One ordinarily rugged man can carry a fairly good size deer by himself. There are two handy ways of accomplishing this. I prefer to drape the animal over my shoulders like a scarf and to hold onto the legs. This way, if you start to slip or stumble, you can get rid of the load in a hurry.

If you've tied it into a pack by lashing the legs together, you may fall and find an uncomfortable amount of weight pressing you down. A common way of carrying deer, nevertheless, is by tying all four legs together and then running your head between body and legs, with the shank ends held down in front of your chest with one hand. The flats on the sides of one fore and one hind leg then rest on your shoulders and do not cut in. It is almost impossible to carry a heavy deer any distance piggyback because of the way the sharp bones bite into the shoulders.

If under any circumstances whatsoever you carry a deer through a forest frequented by other hunters, tie a brightly colored cloth or other red or orange material conspicuously around it. It isn't a bad idea, either, to whistle loudly.

SKINNING. If you are an old-time hunter, you'll very possibly prefer to complete the skinning on the spot. You may pretty well have to do this if your trophy is big. (To make rawhide, see Colonel Townsend Whelen's and my Stackpole book, *On Your Own in the Wilderness*.) There are exceptions, of course, depending generally on the available methods of transportation and to some degree on the weather.

You'll want to get the hide off as soon as reasonably practical. The meat should be allowed to cool thoroughly with the least possible delay. Unless the animal is a small one and is opened wide, it won't cool quickly in temperate weather with the skin on. And if you're in a cold climate, you'll want to be sure to complete the skinning before the hide freezes on, or what would have been a few minutes' work may very easily develop into a cold and disagreeable all-day chore. Besides, bacterial growth is prevented on the surface of the meat when the air can get to it.

To skin a deer, first remove the lower legs or shanks. The novice is likely to begin too high at what most of us think of as the knees. Cut deeply through skin, flesh, and muscle about an inch below these joints. Then brace your knee against what are actually the ankles. Pull forward briskly in the case of a front leg, backward with the hind leg, and the shank will snap off.

Your taxidermist can make very attractive gun and clothes racks, lamps, and other nostalgic items from the shanks with attached hoofs. Skin these all the way down. Cut all meat off the bones but leave the latter attached. Then salt thoroughly and send to the taxidermist, either with instructions or with a request for his suggestions.

Now we come to the actual skinning. Slit the hide along the inside of each leg to meet the belly cut. Extend this latter incision on up to the neck just short of the jaw. Then cut completely around the neck, close behind the jaws, ears, and antlers. If you may want to have the head mounted, however, you proceed a bit differently at this stage, as noted in a moment.

Slit the underside of the tail, also. Then start at each of these cuts in turn to peel the skin from the flesh. If you are working on the ground, use the hide throughout as a clean rug on which to keep the meat unsullied. Generally, the skin will come away neatly, particularly if the animal has just been shot. In places where it adheres rather firmly, such as along the neck, use your knife carefully to cut it loose.

Avoid as much as possible making any nicks in the hide. You will notice between skin and flesh a thin, white film resembling parchment which, as a matter of fact, it is in a sense. Touch this film with a sharp blade, and the skin will continue to peel off. If anyone is helping you, have that individual keep the hide pulled taut while you free it with the long easy sweeps of a keen knife.

Despite all your care, there will be a few places where thin layers of meat and fat will adhere to the skin. When you have the latter off and can find some time to work on it, perhaps leisurely beside the campfire at night, neatly flesh it. One way to make this task easier is to stretch the section on which you are working tightly and comfortably across a knee. Fleshing consists of cutting, scraping, or peeling off all pieces of meat and fat that adhere to the hide.

If a rug is what you want, lace the skin to a frame. Or stretch it, with the hair against a building or a big tree, with nails around the edge. Or, leaving the fleshed side up, stake it out on clean and dry ground by pegs driven around the perimeter through little slits made six inches apart. Let it dry away from moisture and sunshine. If there are blow-flies and bugs around, rub the inside of it with salt to discourage them. A day or so later, wipe the wet salt off and let the skin dry as before.

You may be on the go, however, and unable to stretch the skin. It can still be kept in fine shape for a rug by salting it thoroughly all over the fleshed side, turning the ends and edges in, and rolling the whole thing into a limp bundle that may be stowed in a loose burlap bag if one is handy and hung in a cool dry place. The hide does not have to be fleshed too closely when handled this way.

HEADS FOR MOUNTING. In case your game has excellent antlers and you want to have the head mounted as a trophy, instead of skinning as previously indicated, proceed in this manner. Starting at a point atop the shoulders, slit the hide down over each shoulder until the two incisions meet at the point of the chest between the forelegs. Commencing again at the top of the shoulders, cut forward along the top of the neck to a point just between the two antlers.

From these cuts, peel and skin off the shoulders and neck right up to the skull. Run the point of your knife deeply into the cartilages between the skull and the first vertebra, cutting this junction as free as you can. Then push the head hard one way and then the other, and the skull will break free of the backbone. Now you have the head with the cape attached.

Proceed to turn the skin inside out over the head, first cutting very closely around each antler. Then slice away down in the orifice of each ear, leaving these members on the skin, of course. Skin around the eyes, placing a finger in each to make sure you do not cut the lashes. Then cut to the junction of the upper gums close to the teeth, and in front of the front teeth or gums, leaving the nose on the skin.

Salt the ears, eyeholes, nose, and gums very thoroughly. Roll up the scalp, flesh side to flesh side, and leave it for two days while the salt works in. Then wipe as much wet salt off as possible. Hang up the scalp by the nose to dry in the shade, using a bent stick like a coat hanger. Do not stretch the scalp.

In the meantime, remove all flesh from the skull and the lower jaw. Incidentally, this meat is adjudged by many to be the tastiest on the animal. Using a small stick shaped like a small spoon, remove the brains through the hole where the skull was separated from the backbone. Brains, too, are a fine delicacy, scrambled for instance with eggs as suggested later. Send the dry or nearly dry scalp, the skull with antlers attached, and the lower jaw to your taxidermist.

QUARTERING. Once the carcass is free of the skin, which you have been shifting about so as to keep the meat as clean as possible, quartering will be in order. Unless you intend to save the head, ease the point of your blade deeply into the cartilages between the skull and the first vertebra, severing them as well as you can. Then twist

12-OUNCE PORTABLE SAW WITH 20-INCH BLADE.

the head abruptly in one direction and then in the other, and it will snap free.

With a hatchet, ax, or meat saw, split the bone from the belly cut to the neck. Open the neck on the same line and remove the windpipe and gullet. Then split the backbone from neck to tail. The animal will now be in two halves. Quarter it by dividing each of these halves along the line of the lowest ribs.

You may now wrap these quarters, perhaps rubbed with flour, separately in cheesecloth to discourage pests. Sprinkling black pepper on the flesh will, if necessary, also help to keep blue-bottles and such annoyers off while the meat gets a protective casing over its outside. You will also prob-

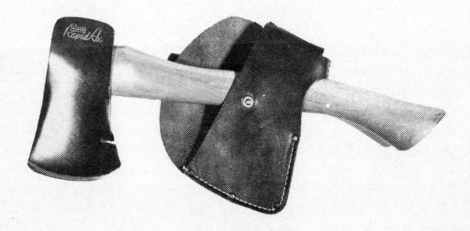

HATCHET.

ably want to examine the meat every day or so to make sure it remains unbothered, giving particular attention to bullet wounds and to folds and nicks in the flesh. Any eggs or larvae so detected can be quickly and harmlessly scraped, wiped, or cut away.

In any event, the quarters can now cool quickly, especially if you hang them high in a tree to hasten the chilling the first night. Some of the pack trains in the mountains, hunting early so as to be back down in the lowlands before snow drifts in too deeply, keep fresh game sweet by trimming the branches out of a tree and pulling the meat high up into the clear 20 feet or more from the ground where blowflies do not operate. Days, the quarters can be wrapped in canvas or bedding to keep them cool.

A meat tent is a handy thing to pack along in hot weather if you have a large enough outfit to warrant its inclusion. A handy model, often seen in work camps in the wilderness, consists of canopied netting with a zipper opening. This shelter is customarily tied in a dark, well ventilated spot by a single rope that runs from its top center.

REFRIGERATION. Keep these quarters as cool and as dry as possible. If you are heading outside, get them into refrigeration as soon as you can. If a long and warm auto trip lies ahead, try at the earliest opportunity both to pack each quarter in a carton of dry ice and to protect those containers in larger ones with crumpled newspapers between for insulation. Circumstances may be such, too, that you'll prefer to travel in the comparative coolness of the night.

If the weather is hot and the distance far, you will probably do well to lay over a day in some locality where you can have the meat frozen solid. This may be a desirable time to cut and wrap it in plainly labeled packages that can be retrieved from the freezer and used one by one. Odd portions can be ground into hamburger, along with a desirable proportion of beef fat unless you object.

It should then be an easy job, with the help of dry ice which these days is obtainable along most routes, to bring these packages frozen to your cold storage cabinet, drawer, locker, or butcher's cold room. You'll have some really fine meat.

FISH

TO CLEAN A FISH. Slit the abdomen from the vent to the neck as soon as possible after catching. Take out the entrails. Scrape the kidney tissue from along the backbone with the knife tip or thumbnail. Some of the sweetest meat is in the head and tail, but if you'd prefer to have them off, sever them with a sharp knife. If you're by a stream, you'll probably rinse the cavity in cold running water. Otherwise, it is preferable to wipe it out well with a clean damp cloth. Keep the fish dry and cool.

TO REMOVE THE FINS. Cut into the flesh on either side of the fin. Then grasp the fin and yank it abruptly toward the head so as to pull out the bones. If you ever trim fins with shears or knife, leave these bones in sight so that they can be dislodged easily after being loosened by cooking.

TO SCALE. Hold the fish firmly on a flat surface. Scrape off the scales with a blunt knife, working swiftly from tail to head. Scales are most easily removed if you can give a few moments to the job while the fish is still wet from the water.

TO SKIN. Slice off a thin ribbon of skin along the entire length of the backbone once the back fins have been removed. Then loosen the skin around the gills. Grasp the skin, finally, and peel it from head to tail. With tough hides like that of the ling, pliers are handy. Turn the fish over and do the same thing on the other side.

TO FILLET. Cut down from the head to the tail, along the backbone, with a sharp pointed knife. Turn the knife flat and cut the flesh along the spine to the tail, letting the knife slide over the ribs. Lift off the side of the fish in one piece. Turn the fish over and remove the other fillet the same way. Fillets are those slices, boneless or nearly so, cut lengthwise along the ribs parallel to the backbone. Steaks, on the other hand, are slabs cut at right angles to the backbone.

TO BONE. Lay the fish on its side and with a sharp pointed knife cut from the head to the tail close to the spine. Turn the fish on its other side and make a similar cut. Sever the head if this hasn't already been done. Then carefully lift out the entire backbone. Pick out as many remaining small bones as possible.

TO KEEP FISH IN CAMP. Clean immediately after catching, wipe dry, and then put in a dry nest of grass or other green vegetation within a creel or similar container. Completely surround each fish with the grass or such, so that no fish touches another. The top layer of vegetation may be moistened slightly, inasmuch as evaporation will make for added coolness. But no more dampness should touch the fish. Keep them cool, dry, and clean.

KEEPING FISH. One way to keep such fish several days without refrigeration is to swathe the fish and vegetation in a lot of newspapers, early in the morning after they have been chilled by the night air. Then pick a spot that will remain shaded all day and bury the package underground. Or the package can be rolled during the day in dampened burlap or such, then laid out each night to air and cool.

Another method is to wrap each fish, sprinkled with salt or corn meal if you want, in wax paper after it has been cleaned and dried. Then roll in dry fabric or newspaper and wrap a second time. Sacking or other material may then be soaked, wrung out, and then lashed over the dry bundle with each end roped tight. Keep in as cool a place as possible, preferably away from open air. Do not open until the fish are to be used. This bundle can be successfully shipped in a box with ice, providing that the ice does not touch the fish.

Green grass or similar vegetation can also be used to insulate fish that are to be shipped with ice. Pad the bottom of a wooden box thickly with grass or similar green vegetation. Wrap each fish separately in more greens or in paper and nest them in the box, covering them with additional vegetation. Lay a quantity of large sheets of paper over the box, flatten their centers down across the fish, cover with some four to six inches of ice, then fold up and over the ice. Place more paper on top, nail on the cover, and plainly mark, "This Side Up, Perishable Fish."

Fish can also be tastily smoked, dried, or preserved by methods detailed in my Stackpole Company book, *How To Go Live in the Woods on $10 a Week*.

GAME BIRDS

For best results, unless you have preferences to the contrary, remove the crop and entrails as soon as possible. This may often be successfully delayed for a few hours, but if the bird is badly shot up, the flavor of the meat is apt to be affected. Also, such dressing, in the opinion of many of us, desirably hastens the cooling process.

The crop is situated loosely beneath the skin at the base of the throat. Slit open the skin, take it out, and pull out the windpipe.

Then make a crosswise slit below the breastbone. With small birds that are not going to be stuffed, you can often just hold the legs in one hand, the breast in the other, and pull the bird open. Reach into the abdominal cavity and carefully draw out the insides. Cut out the vent. Then wipe the bird dry. Do not leave any blood clots on the interior.

Save the liver, gizzard, and heart. Very gently cut out the little gall bladder intact and discard it. Its contents are so bitter that any dark portions where they may have spilled on the liver may well be cut from this delicacy as well. Clean the gizzard by easing the knife through to the hard center, then pulling the flesh away from this central sac.

Before using you may remove the oil sac at the base of the tail, disjoint the legs below the thighs, and cut off the head.

Birds should be cooled as quickly as possible. Separating them rather than piling them into a hot game pocket will speed this. If allowed to hang in a cool place soon after they have been shot and drawn, a protective glaze will be formed from contact with the air. They should be kept cool until used. Flavor will be better if they are hung for at least several days before being used.

To save yourself work and to avoid tearing the skin, dry pluck the fowl while it is still warm. Remaining pinfeathers may be removed with the fingernails or with tweezers. Singe the down off quickly, being careful not to burn the skin. Do not pass the bird through the flames of a lighted newspaper, however, as the ink has a blackening effect.

Birds may be plucked later, of course. Scalding is then recommended for grouse, pheasant, quail, and similar fowl. Hold the bird by the feet and quickly plunge it several times into hot, not boiling water, until the feathers loosen readily. Scalding waterfowl, however, usually makes the plucking even more difficult and results in loss of flavor.

Small duck, coot, and such may as well be skinned. Just slit open the back. Pulling in opposite directions with both hands if you want, peel off the skin like a glove. Cut off head, wings, and feet.

Despite a loss in flavor, many hunters skin other birds rather than bother plucking them. As a matter of fact, how you handle your game birds is decided by your own palate. Each of us is a gourmet in his own right.

SMALL GAME

Clean, skin, and cool as soon as possible. Remove any scent or musk glands if they do not come off with the hide. These small, waxy or reddish kernels or glands, located under the forelegs and along the spine or under the lower part of the abdomen, often pull away with the skin. Cut out all imbedded glands, removing them intact if possible so as not to give a musky flavor to the meat.

If you can handle big game, you'll have no trouble with small meat animals. Matter of fact, if you're not going to save the skin, just ring it with your knife around the middle part of the body. Pull half toward the head and the other half toward the tail. Cut off the head, feet, and tail, and that's that. Fur animals deserve more pains. Complete, detailed directions for handling these are to be found in the Stackpole book, *On Your Own in the Wilderness.*

Rabbit and certain other small game are susceptible to infections that can be passed on to man. These are less likely to exist after the first heavy frost and during cold weather. One precaution is to pass up all but lively game. The prudent hunter will also take particular pains to avoid cutting himself while handling any small game and will don rubber or plastic gloves whenever he has any cuts or wounds on his hands. Thorough washing of the hands with a strong soap, followed by the use of a disinfectant after dressing the game, will vastly reduce the danger of any infection.

The liver of each animal, the rabbit especially, should be examined for possible infection. The liver of a healthy animal is clear, dark red in color, firm, and unspotted. Small white cystlike spots, the size of peas or smaller, may indicate the presence of tularemia. Germs of this, incidentally, are destroyed by thorough cooking. But the thing to do when you are aware of its presence, of course, is to burn or deeply bury the infected carcass. Painstaking cleansing of the hands is essential after an infected carcass has been handled.

Thoroughly cooked meat, it may be repeated, is completely safe. By observing the above few simple rules for handling freshly killed small game animals, and by cooking the meat until well done, danger of contracting tularemia from infected animals is removed; one reason why more wild rabbits continue to be happily taken by hunters each year on this continent than any other game, large or small.

CHAPTER 4

FAME WITH BIG GAME

What too many well-meaning cooks do to big game meat shouldn't happen in a nightmare. The result? The hunter is crestfallen. The cook feels unappreciated. A lot of top-notch grub is wasted.

More game meat is ruined by overcooking than by any other misadventure. The major reasons for this are two. The cook has the mistaken opinion that an abundance of heat is the way to assure tenderness. There is also the erroneous notion that high temperatures will burn away the wild flavor.

If your deer or moose tastes best to you rare, that's fine. If not, there's still a way around. Overcooking is ordinarily fatal to most big game, with the exception of bear, because of its general lack of the layers of fat common to comparable domestic meats. Such wild meat dries out under heat, and the fibers quickly tend to harden and toughen. An antidote? A non-seasoned meat tenderizer. For best results with game, use more than the instructions suggest and let it stand a shorter time.

Whether or not some people like a particular game meat largely depends on their taste prejudices. In other words, individuals sit down for the first time to deer that's kept sassy on willow shoots, and they expect it to taste like corn-fattened beef. It doesn't. The instinctive reaction, no matter how delicious the venison may be in its own right? Unfavorable.

Such taste prejudices can work themselves out in a while, when repeated servings begin to assume a familiar taste. There are better ways around, however. One of these short-cuts is to present the meat in as favorable an aspect as possible, surrounded with familiar and favorite side dishes, especially the impressionable first time.

Most of the other methods have to do with actually reducing any objectionable wild game flavors. These latter efforts start in the field with immediate cleaning and rapid cooling, as already considered. They continue with proper handling and storage. When the meat reaches the cooking area, there is an even wider range of choices. Among them are the following general methods, often used both with modifications and in combination.

Cut and pull off all loose fat, inasmuch as this carries most of the game's flavor. Replace this, if at all possible, with beef fat. Your meat man, or any cattle raiser who's been butchering, will sell you a large bag full for a quarter, and it can make all the difference. While you're in the woods, other fat will do, of course. The whiteness or yellowness of fat, incidentally, is no indication of quality or age. Yellow fat merely indicates that the carotin, the yellow substance found in all vegetation, has not yet been converted to Vitamin A.

Trim the meat well before using it, removing all discolored and dehydrated portions and especially any hard or dry outer husk.

You can use spices, herbs, sauces, and the like if you want to alter or modify flavor. The trouble is that you're apt to get too far from the natural deliciousness of game meat. A more natural method? Plain, ordinary bouillon cubes, beef extracts, and similar preparations.

There's this, too. Roasts and stews will have far fewer unfamiliar flavors than steaks. As for such delicacies as heart and liver, these can seldom be distinguished from those bought at the butcher shop.

Finally, if you want, you may soak the meat overnight in a solution of vinegar, water, and spices. Some cooks employ wines, combinations of oil and weak acids such as lemon and tomato juice, barbecue sauces, and the like.

Most of us who love the woods prefer fine game meat quickly cooked, on the rare side, with only salt, pepper, and melting butter or margarine to bring out the delectable natural flavors. However, for one reason or another usually having to do either with age or mating, some meat is below average in savor. Also, everyone is a gourmet in his own right. If an individual prefers to marinate either a prime slab of beef or an equally choice moose sirloin, who is to say that he is wrong?

For those who may be interested, here is a better than usual marinade that will flavor and tenderize some 7 or 8 pounds of steak cut no less than 1½ inches thick. This marinade can be prepared at home by blending the following: 2 tablespoons olive oil, ½ cup wine vinegar, 1 rounded teaspoon oregano, and a sparsely measured ⅛ teaspoon apiece of salt, black pepper, Italian red pepper, and cayenne pepper. When ready to use, pour this into a flat dish where it will lie about ½ inch deep. Immerse the meat about suppertime, topping it with a thinly sliced medium-size onion and covering the dish. Turn the meat once the last thing at night. The steaks will be ready the next day.

This will give a general idea. Actually, if you taste occasionally, use a certain degree of restraint, and have the inclination, you can usually concoct an adequate marinade from the materials at hand. A virtually foolproof wild game marinade can be made, for example, by diluting a cheap red wine such as a claret with half its volume of water, then returning its authority by adding small amounts of pepper, bay leaf, rosemary, tarragon, thyme, mustard seed— anything that gives a pleasing taste.

WHAT TO EAT FIRST

The first parts of the big game animal to eat, while the body of the meat is taking on flavor and tenderness with age, include the liver, heart, kidneys, brains, and tongue. If you don't utilize at least most of these, you're passing up some mighty fine feasting.

LIVER. Slice about ½ inch thick. Brown in a heavy frypan in bacon drippings or other fat until done to taste. Include onions and bacon by all means if you want. Liver is best when it is kept on the rare side. Overcooking gives you a tough, dry, tasteless, and far less nutritious product.

Grilled liver beats the frypan product four ways from go. This is one reason why, if you're hungry by the time you've collected that deer, bear, or sheep, you may choose to emulate the Indian hunter. If so, build a small fire and drape the liver, or slices of it, over a rack made of green wood. Or just shove a pointed stick into the ground and impale the liver on it, turning it occasionally in any event. It will not take long to cook. Fresh liver is delicious without seasoning, although if you want you can do like many sportsmen and always carry a small container of salt.

Liver sliced an inch or so thick and briefly grilled over an open fire until crisp outside and pinkly juicy within is delectable. Cutting into the meat will show you when it is ready. Butter liberally just before serving.

HEART. Brown the heart in natural fat or shortening in a dutch oven. Season with salt and pepper. Then set the heart on a rack. Pour in a cup of boiling water. Cover and pot roast slowly in an oven or atop the heat for about 20 minutes per pound; only until the meat cuts easily. It should be rare to be tender. If you prefer yours well done, it is well to help it along with one of the tenderizers. Too much heat will otherwise give you a dry chunk of leather. Add more boiling water if necessary. Peeled onions, carrots, potatoes, and such may be put in toward the end. Basting the heart every half hour seems to improve the flavor. It certainly stimulates the appetite.

Big game hearts are also excellent broiled over cooking coals. Cut into thin slices, season, baste with butter or margarine, and cook about 3 minutes to a side. Eat while still sizzling. A tart jam or marmalade served on the side makes these taste even better. So does a kettle of hot black tea steeping within arm's reach.

KIDNEYS. "If I could eat just once more, I'd sure pick bear kidneys," King Gething told me up on the headwaters of the Peace River. "I'd want them simmered awhile with butter, salt, cloves, celery if I had any, and a mite of onion. Matter of fact, let's get 'em on the fire before somebody else shows up."

Cut or divide the kidneys into segments about the size of chicken hearts. All you have to do with bear kidneys to achieve this is strip away the connective membrane. Let the kidneys and other ingredients simmer in low heat until tender. Best way to establish proportions is by taste. These kidneys are especially tasty atop either steaming mountains of mashed potato or hot crusty bannock, streaming with butter or margarine.

BRAINS. This one is worth the trouble. It's also a practical way of reminding yourself how small and precisely positioned a target the brain of a big game animal actually is. Best way in is with a meat saw, although a battered woodpile bludgeon will get the job done. If you have a dog along, wire the head loosely to a tree, so he won't bury and forget it, and he'll worry away happily at it for as long as you're in camp.

Remove the outer membrane of the brains. Dip them in beaten egg, roll in cracker or bannock crumbs seasoned with salt and pepper, and saute uncovered in butter or margarine. These have a delicate flavor and go well with scrambled eggs.

If you haven't any fresh eggs in camp, however, immerse the brains in melted butter or margarine and then crumbs. Pan broil slowly until crisp outside and hot throughout. Serve with buttered toast, hot biscuits, or boiled potatoes.

MARROW BONES. "They can keep them filly-minions and sech," an old prospector told me once over coffee in Seattle. "Me, I'm heading back to where I can knock over a caribou. I'd roast me the tongue first, except the liver is durned near as good and won't keep so long. I ain't forgetting the leg bones, either. Ever heat them in your campfire, then bust them open with rocks to get at the marrow? Then you savvy what I'm palavering about."

Marrow bones from any of the large game animals are an epicurean's delight.

TONGUE. Tongue is another delicacy you shouldn't let get by you. Those from the larger animals are special tidbits, that from a moose being as big as a beef tongue.

Caribou tongue is also excellent. So is elk tongue. The only drawback to that from the usual deer is its small size.

In case you've heretofore passed up this choice bit, there's a trick to securing it. Feel for the bones under the lower jaw. Make a deep slit between them up into the mouth. Press the tongue down through this opening. Grasp and cut off as close to the base as possible.

Cover with cold, salted water. Bring to a boil. Spoon off any scum that has come to the surface. Then simmer until the tongue is tender. When it has cooled sufficiently in the stock to permit its being handled easily, skin it. A sharp knife will help, although much of the skin can be peeled off with the fingers alone. Remove any small bones at the base.

This meat is especially good thinly sliced, either hot or cold. If you want something special, smoke the cooked and peeled tongue over a smudge of ground birch, alder, willow, or similar hardwood for several hours.

MOOSE MUFFLE. The moose is far and away the heftiest game animal in this hemisphere that is widely hunted for its meat. Polar bear and grizzly grow bigger, it's true, but neither is famous for steaks. Moose meat is something else again. To put it briefly, it has been my main sustenance for a double handful of winters in the Far North, and by choice.

All that Horace Kephart said about this particular part (moose muffle), though, was: "Boil like a pig's head. Add an onion."

More bafflingly, as far as my schoolboy knowledge was concerned when I first read these brief instructions, he called it moose muffle. That made me think of the woolen muffler I wound around my neck in snowy New England weather, which in turn brought my conjectures to the moose's bell. It was some Crees, years later, who straightened me out. I'm happy they did, for if you, too, ever get a chance to eat any, moose muzzle is something you shouldn't miss.

I've roasted this delicacy before an open birch fire, picked out with my knife point what I could devour of the meat, and given the remainder to my 180-pound Irish wolfhound who was along as a packdog.

A more conservative method, after you've cut off the upper jaw just below the eyes, is to drop it into a large kettle of scalding water and parboil it an hour. Remove and cool in cold water. Pluck out the loosened hairs and wash.

Then put the moose muzzle in fresh water along with some onions, salt, and pepper. Simmer until tender. Then set away from the heat. After the muffle has cooled in its juice, extract bone and cartilage.

You'll end up with the white meat from the bulb of the muzzle and dark strips from along bone and jowls. Cut these into slices. What you don't eat on the spot, pack into a handy container and cover with the juice. This will jell. When chilled, the jellied moose muzzle can be profitably sliced for eating cold.

BROILING. Townsend Whelen and I were reminiscing just the other day about different wild American meats we have eaten—south through Mexico to Panama, all the way across the original 48 States, northeast to New Brunswick and Nova Scotia and Hudson Bay, and northwest into British Columbia and the Yukon to Alaska.

That involves considerable feasting. But I went all the way with the Colonel when he summed it up like this: "I do think that there is no better way to cook the meat of large animals than to broil it over the coals of an outdoor wood fire.

"When I was a boy there was a very excellent artist named Tappan Adney whose specialty was depicting the Indians of our Northwest. I so well remember one painting of his of a group of Siwash Indians cooking meat before a fire. Chunks of meat, alternating large and small, were impaled on a stick that was leaned over and towards the blaze. Way back in 1901 in British Columbia I spent several days in camp with an old mountain man and his klutch (squaw). They had just killed a ewe, and that night she cooked it in just the same way.

"She impaled large chunks of lean meat about the size

of baseballs, alternating with chunks of fat about as large as a golf ball, on a thin green stick about two feet long, and sticking one end of this stick in the ground alongside the fire, she leaned the stick over towards the blaze exactly as Tappan Adney had depicted it. Then she turned the stick every couple of minutes until the chunks were pretty well charred on the outside, but still almost raw in the center. I have never since tasted such delicious meat in my whole life. Since then I have always cooked my venison in that way when I had the opportunity."

As long as I can remember, I've used a modified version of this at noon when I have stopped to boil the kettle; threading inch-square chunks of already salted game meat onto a sharpened green stick, thrusting them briefly into the blaze to form a juice-restraining glaze, and then broiling them a few minutes in the fringes of the heat. These I bite off one by one to punctuate alternating mouthfuls of hot toasted sandwich. Choice cut for these kabobs among the really big game? The filet mignon; that is, the small end of the tenderloin. When you get through these and the rest of the tenderloins, move to the back steaks.

BROILED SPARERIBS. Indian hunters improvise racks in the reflected heat of campfires by sticking a few roughly trimmed green limbs in the ground and laying smaller sticks between the crotches. Over these they drape hastily hacked rib sections to sputter and sizzle while they're finishing dressing out the animal. Or sometimes they just shove a spread of ribs onto a single slanted stake. Charred a bit, all these taste fine without seasoning.

A more conservative way to come by the same delicacy in camp is to saw chunks of the rib area into serving pieces. Place on a greased, preheated rack over the coals. Turning occasionally, cook for about 20 minutes or until the ribs are crisp and brown. Then you'll probably want to salt and pepper, or to spice up some catsup if you're a barbecue fancier and season with that. In any event, big game ribs may well be used a few days before steaks and roasts, as they're susceptible to drying out and, when fat, to picking up off flavors.

SWEET AND SOUR SPARERIBS. Saw some 2 pounds of ribs into serving portions. Brown in a frypan over moderate heat about 5 minutes on each side. Add ½ cup water, ¼ cup raisins, and ½ teaspoon salt. Cover pan tightly and cook over very low heat 20 minutes. Add two sliced green peppers if you have them; a similar bulk of some other green such as celery, wild mustard leaves, watercress, peas, etc. if you don't.

Blend 1½ tablespoons of cornstarch with 1¼ cup sugar, 1¼ cup vinegar, and 1 cup of water. Mix this with the other ingredients in the pan. Re-cover and continue cooking over low heat for another 1½ hours. Stir occasionally and if necessary add more water to prevent drying. Before serving, perhaps with rice, sprinkle on soy sauce if possible. I most always keep some of this latter in my outfit. If you've never tried it, you'll better appreciate why when you discover the elusively different flavor a few drops give such wilderness dishes as cold venison and boiled wild greens.

BAKED VENISON CHOPS. Arrange four thick chops in an open baking pan. Measure out a cup of canned tomato, using the solid portions. Spoon this over the chops. Then distribute a sliced onion atop the meat. Salt and pepper.

Pour in a cup of water and bake in a moderately hot oven for 45 minutes. Turn the chops once. Another 30 minutes should see them tender and ready to serve, perhaps along with mashed potatoes into each serving of which a spoonful of the juice is depressed. If they've had this before, you'll only have to call them once for dinner.

STEAKS. These are always best over an open fire. Even when I'm surrounded on four sides by log walls, as admitted in *How To Go Live in the Woods On $10 a Week,* during reasonably warm weather we still take to the outdoors to broil steaks over hot wood coals. Cooler days we often open the cabin windows, remove a lid from the wood stove, and cook in a similar fashion. How about when temperatures get a snapping 60° below? The only difference is that the windows stay closed.

The rest of the time I mostly pan broil all top grade steaks, cutting them 2½ inches thick, quickly searing both

sides in a hot and preferably heavy frypan, and then cooking with slightly less heat until done to taste. Salt the metal
well before putting the meat in and have it really hot. No
grease at all is used, and that sputtering from the meat is
tipped out. Salt and pepper if you want, and daub with butter
or margarine after cooking. Serve on preheated plates.

Cooking over open embers is still unbeatable, however. A
good trick at the start is to get a glowing bed of coals, then
to sprinkle on a few chips and shavings. These will flare up
enough both to help seal in the juices and to give that flavor-
some char relished by so many. As you're already aware, the
grill should be greased beforehand to prevent sticking. A
handy one for wilderness use? One of those lightweight
campfire grates available from most large outfitters. Removing the folding wire legs will make for easier packing
if that's any problem. It's a simple matter to lay such a grid
between logs or rocks.

Individual steaks can also be very pleasingly grilled merely
by holding them over the heat by means of sturdy, forked
green sticks.

Lean meat cooks more quickly than fat meat. Aging also
progressively shortens the cooking time. Then there are such
factors as size, shape, and the amount of bone. Outdoor
fires add another variable. A practical way to test is to prick
the steak with a sharpened stick. If red juice wells out, the
meat is rare; pink, medium rare; colorless, overdone unless
that is the way you want it.

SWISS GAME STEAK. This is good both for a change
and for those days when you're confronted with the tougher
cuts. Flank handled this way will work into a tasty steak
of sorts. Slitting such game meat every few inches along the
trimmed edges will keep it from curling unduly.

For about a 3-pound slab, mix 2 teaspoons salt with ½
teaspoon black pepper. Season one side of the steak with
half of this. Then with the back of your camping knife pound
all the flour you can into the meat. Turn the steak and repeat both processes.

Melt 5 tablespoons of bacon drippings, bear grease, lard,

margarine, or the like in a dutch oven or in a large skillet which has a cover. Quickly brown the meat all over.

Then spread a large onion and an equal bulk of carrot, diced together, over the steak. Add a can of tomatoes. Cover and simmer over low heat 1½ hours. Then bank the meat with enough small, peeled potatoes for the ensuing meal. Cook for an additional half hour or until the potatoes are tender.

ROASTS. Tender big game roasts are best cooked rare so as to take fullest advantage of the natural savor of the meat. If the meat isn't tender, treat first with one of the unseasoned commercial tenderizers.

Moderately slow oven temperatures give the best results with the large roasts. About 12 minutes per pound should do it, to give you an idea. Searing, inasmuch as it keeps in no juices, is unnecessary. If one side of the meat is fattest, placing this uppermost will give you the energy-conserving advantage of some natural basting. Laying strips of beef fat over venison or similar roasts, or pinning on chunks of such fat with small whittled skewers, will vastly improve the final results. Meat should be left uncovered, salted beforehand if you want but not floured, and cooked without any addition of water.

The reflector baker does a particularly wonderful job in this department. Turn the roast occasionally to encourage uniform cooking. While you're at it, scrub enough potatoes for the meal. Slice off the ends to allow steam to escape. Rub with shortening or cooking oil. Place in the oven to cook along with the roast.

BUFFALO POT ROAST. Buffalo are occasionally legal game in Alaska and in the vicinity of Great Slave Lake in Canada. Tougher portions of the meat, which tastes like a heavy beef, cook up well as pot roasts. This same recipe for sort of a super-speed sauerbraten will also give you a change with other big game. For a 7- or 8-pound chunk, preferably in the case of a buffalo chunk shot through with orangish lines of fat, you'll need:

    3 tablespoons shortening
    1½ tablespoons vinegar

>   1 tablespoon cinnamon
>   1 tablespoon ginger
>   1 teaspoon nutmeg
>   1 tablespoon salt
>   ¼ teaspoon pepper
>   1½ cups water
>   3 cups apple juice
>   1 can condensed tomato soup
>   1 cup chopped onion
>   1 teaspoon chopped garlic (optional)
>   flour

Melt the shortening in the bottom of a dutch oven and brown the meat atop the stove. Blend the vinegar, cinnamon, ginger, nutmeg, salt, and pepper. Add the water and apple juice, that from cooked dried apples being excellent. Pour over the meat. Spoon the concentrated tomato soup, the onion, and if you want some garlic atop the roast.

Cover and cook in enough heat to keep the pot simmering for 4 hours or until the roast is tender. Thicken the gravy with flour and clear a way to the table.

"BOILED" MEAT. Cut the meat into about 2-inch cubes. Drop these individually into just enough bubbling water to cover. Do not boil. Don't salt until almost ready to serve. Meat so cooked can best be relished after it has been simmering covered only 5 minutes or so. However, many get the habit of letting it cook an hour or more.

Often rice and other vegetables, particularly onions, are cooked along with the meat to make what is often called mulligan. The addition of any such components, except when included for flavor only, should be so staggered that everything will be done at the same time. Any extra fluid should be heated before it is added.

If you are going to use the meat cold, let it cool in the broth. For a taste treat with moose and caribou eaten this way, try sprinkling a little soy sauce over it and serving wild berry jam on the side.

The dutch oven will conveniently so "boil" a big solid chunk of game meat. Place the meat in the bottom of the oven along with onions if you have any, perhaps a sliced carrot or two, and 1½ teaspoons of salt per pound. Half cover the meat with simmering water. Cook about an hour for every pound, at the end of which time the meat should be tender but not stringy or mushy. If you want to use it in cold sandwiches, let it cool in the broth. Then move to a flat utensil that will also hold a little of the broth. Press it into shape with a weighted cover or plate so that it can later be more handily sliced.

MULLIGAN. The preceding is the basis of the stew called mulligan. What the end result of this staple will be depends more or less on ingenuity, imagination, and the materials at hand. Available vegetables go well in such a stew. So do odds and ends of steaks and roasts.

When a lot of us are off by ourselves, the tendency is to go in for one-dish meals. This we can easily accomplish with such mulligans, even to the extent of making bread unnecessary by adding a starch such as rice, potatoes, noodles, macaroni, one of the cooked cereals, or perhaps a steaming soft dome of dumplings.

PACK TRAIN MULLIGAN. This trail mulligan is a favorite of some of the cooks on big game hunting parties when their pack trains make camp late after a long ride. Cut 3 pounds of caribou or other game meat into inch squares. Brown with 2 tablespoons of margarine or lard in the bottom of a stew pail. Then put in 2 quarts of water and 1 tablespoon of salt. Cover and boil until the meat is done.

Add hot water as necessary to bring the water back to its original level. Add 1½ cups macaroni, spaghetti, noodles, or the like. When this is nearly soft enough to eat, put in two large (15 oz.) cans of chili con carne or anything of the sort that may be handy in an accessible pannier. Salt and pepper to taste. Cook only a few minutes, just long enough for the mulligan to thicken. Serve with piping hot bannock. And if you want seconds yourself, you'd better get your refill in a hurry.

STEWING. Stew meat, which can be the toughest in the critter, is best browned at the onset with fat, chopped onion, and seasonings in the bottom of the kettle. You can then if you want stir in enough flour to make a thick smooth gravy.

For liquid, use any fluid in which vegetables have been cooked or canned, broth from boiled meat, or water. Season to taste, bring to a bubble, and then place tightly covered where it will simmer all morning or all afternoon.

A dutch oven is a handy receptacle for stew inasmuch as you can dig a hole, always in a safe place where fire can not spread, and leave it buried there among hot coals while you spend the day hiking, fishing, or hunting.

BEAR. When I was writing *Living off the Country* for the Stackpole Company, I tasted every kind of wild meat that I could come by handily—wolf, lynx, cougar, muskrat, beaver, and so on, together with moose, caribou, antelope, and the like. I also sampled opinions. Those who dine on bear meat fairly often, I found, are almost unanimously agreed that the North American wilderness affords no more delicious game with the single exception of mountain sheep, and the last is only the best meat, wild or tame, I've ever eaten anywhere.

Many hunters, most of whom have never tasted bear meat nor smelled it cooking, are prejudiced against the carnivore as food for one reason or another. One reason often heard concerns the animal's eating habits. Yet the most ravenous bear is a finicky diner when compared to such delicacies as lobster and chicken.

It's true enough that not even a plump young yearling furnishes really good steaks, which is where many culinary attempts end. But even an oldster big enough to carpet a cabin will cook up into roasts and stews so moist and savory that you have to eat them to believe them. The meat then so resembles top grade beef that you can serve it as such to individuals who've vowed they'd never touch bear meat and actually have them coming back for second and third helpings. I've seen more than one convert made that way.

And the mulligans? Well, if bear weren't such good eating, I'd have given up hunting them after collecting my first two or three.

Any excess fat should be trimmed off before the meat is

cooked. This fat may then be heated in open pans to extract the grease. Strained into jars, that of the black bear hardens into a clear white solid that makes the best shortening that any user I've talked to has ever come across. That procured from a grizzly is also excellent and, when similarly rendered, remains a more easily measured oil. Both are prized in the farther places for everything from medicine to mixing with molasses for Yankee butter.

BROTH. When trophy hunting in pack horse country, you sometimes find yourself back of beyond with more good game meat than you can ever hope to bring out. Maybe you'll delay in camp a few days longer. Still, you can scarcely begin to eat it.

On occasions like this, why not really splurge on broth and enjoy all you possibly can? What I've done such times is get the kettle simmering, hang a ladle nearby, and let everyone help himself until the pot is exhausted. Then begin another. Thing to remember is that the liquid will boil down, so don't get it too salty at the start.

Just cut the meat into small pieces so that you'll get the most good out of it. Shot portions are fine. So are all lesser cuts that you haven't time or room to handle otherwise. Marrow bones, split or sawed, are unequalled. Those necks and backs of game birds can be used this way, too. Add about 1 cup of cold water for every ½ pound of meat and bone. Cover and simmer (not boil) upwards of 4 hours.

Incidentally, if you get hungry between meals, the meat itself is wonderful hot and swimming in melting butter or margarine.

SOUP. Start like the above. In fact, you can ladle out what broth you need for the liquid part of the soup. If the broth you want to use for the soup has somehow become too salty, let it simmer along with some raw potatoes. Then remove the potatoes. Gently saute in the bottom of the kettle whatever vegetables you're going to use. Figure out your times so that these will not be overcooked. (See the chapter on vegetables.) Then add the broth and cover. Do not boil or you'll spoil the flavor. Do not season until 5 minutes before you're ready to serve.

CAMP HASH. When you have cold vegetables left over and maybe not enough cooked meat to go around, here is a solution. Cut the venison or other meat up fine. If you're a bit short on meat, help the flavor along with a bouillon cube. Add enough chopped vegetables, usually potatoes mostly, to go around. Season to taste.

Be melting several tablespoons of fat in a frypan. If rawish onions bother anyone in the party, cook these first until thoroughly soft. Otherwise, chop up whatever amount you want and mix them with the other ingredients.

Press the hash down into the pan. Cook over slow heat until a crust has formed on the bottom. Fold over and serve while hot.

OTHER METHODS. There are other ways to cook big game meat: baking in a pit, steaming in a hole, baking in clay, baking in the hide, cooking with the help of hot stones in a hollow made by pressing the hide into a small depression scooped in the ground, suspending by a variety of methods over the open fire, roasting in ashes, boiling in bark dishes, etc. Unless you happened to be in the wilderness without cooking utensils, though, you wouldn't ordinarily use most of them once in a decade. Those who are interested in learning more about such primitive and elementary cooking methods, however, will find many of them discussed in my survival book, *Living off the Country.*

SUPPOSE SOME'S LEFT OVER?

PRESERVING MEAT. If you're camping in one place and have a quantity of fresh meat you'd like to preserve with a minimum of trouble, cut it into forearm-size strips, following the membranous divisions among the muscles as much as possible. Pull off as much of this parchment as you reasonably can.

Roll the pieces in a mixture made proportionately of 3 pounds of table salt, 4 tablespoons of allspice, and 5 tablespoons of black pepper. Rubbing this well into the meat, then shaking off any excess, will give the best results.

You can either drape the strips over a wire or similar

support, well away from any animals, or you suspend them there after first piercing an end of each with a knife and looping in a string or wire. The treated meat must be kept dry. If you have to travel, rehang it after reaching your destination. About one month is needed for it to shrink and absorb the seasoning properly; less in dry country and more in damp regions. Sliced thin, it's then really something to chew on raw. Scraped and trimmed some, and soaked overnight if you want, it also goes well in mulligan. Game meat so cured is still delicious after several decades, as I can personally testify.

JERKY. The simplest way to preserve meat is by drying it. When this is done most advantageously, it's also one of the most delicious methods. Try some of the beef jerky available in many markets if you have any doubts. And note the price. The amount charged for two or three slim, blackened strips of this dehydrated meat will often buy a good steak.

There's nothing complicated about making jerky. You cut lean deer, moose, elk, caribou, buffalo, and similar red meat into long straps about ½ inch thick. These you hang apart from one another in the sun, in the attic, or some other place where, kept dry, they will gradually lose most of their water content. At the same time, they'll become hard, dry, black and, incidentally, both nourishing and tasty.

The strips may be first soaked, if you want, either in brine or sea water. If you are along the sea coast, you may care to try the ancient method of boiling down ocean water until it becomes extremely salty. While it is still bubbling, immerse a few straps at a time for 3 minutes apiece. If there is no convenient place to hang this meat, it can be laid across sun-warmed rocks and turned every hour or so. You can also make your own brine by dissolving all the salt possible in boiling water.

After the meat has been allowed to drain, some makers sprinkle it with pepper. In many cases they also add favorite spices such as oregano, marjoram, basil, and thyme for increased flavor. Good? Friends of ours in New Mexico and California, with plenty of empty space in their freezers, jerk a deer or so a year in this fashion just for their own personal eating.

A common bush technique for jerking game meat involves draping the strips, or hanging them by string or wire loops, on a wood framework about 4 to 6 feet off the ground. A small, slow, smoky fire of any nonresinous wood is built beneath this rack. The meat is allowed to dry for several days in the sun and wind. It is covered at night and during any rain. The chief use of the fire is to discourage flies and other insects. It should not be hot enough to cook the meat at all.

When jerked, the meat will be hard and more or less black outside. It will keep almost indefinitely away from damp and flies. This covered wagon staple is best eaten as is. Just bite off a chunk and chew. It may also be cooked in stews. It is very concentrated and nourishing, and a little goes a long way as an emergency ration. Alone, it is not a good food for long continued consumption, as it lacks the necessary fat.

The fat, which would turn rancid, should be trimmed off before the drying operation is commenced. It may then be rendered for future use in cooking or in the manufacture of pemmican.

REAL PEMMICAN. Some frightful conglomerations appear on the market from time to time under the name of "pemmican." One which I recently sampled looked and tasted like spoiled fruit cake, this despite a price in excess of 20¢ per ounce.

To make real pemmican, one of the best concentrated foods ever, you begin by pounding up a quantity of jerky. Then take raw animal fat and cut it into walnut-size hunks. Try these out in a pan in the oven or over a slow fire, never letting the grease boil up. Pour the resulting hot fat over the shredded jerky, mixing the two together until you have about the consistency of ordinary sausage. Then pack the pemmican in commercial casings or waterproof bags. Despite some practices, no salt at all should be included. Dried berries? Suit yourself. Their function is as a flavor only.

The ideal proportions of lean and fat in pemmican is, by

weight, approximately equal amounts of well-dried lean meat and rendered fat. It takes approximately 5 pounds of fresh lean meat to make 1 pound of jerky suitable for pemmican.

Such genuine pemmican will afford practically every necessary food element with the exception of Vitamin C. The average individual can get along without this vitamin for at least two months if in good health to begin with. Furthermore, supplementing the pemmican with some fresh food (for example, just several fresh rose hips daily) will supply all the Vitamin C necessary to prevent any trouble with scurvy over even an extended period.

MAKING IT LAST. There are other standard ways of preserving game meat. For instance, I've salt-cured some flat slabs of grizzly, then smoked them. Served up with sourdough hotcakes and scrambled eggs, mornings while the northern lights still fired the sky, the crisp slices never lasted long.

Also, if you find yourself at all interested in canning game animals and birds to help spread the supply deliciously throughout the year—or in making your own sausage, or in smoking or corning meat—these subjects are covered in minute detail in my book, *How To Go Live in the Woods on $10 a Week*. You can almost hear creaking wheels of covered wagon trains when you eat grub like this.

CHAPTER 5

BIRDS AND SMALL GAME

Meat is the one complete food. To put it another way, plump fresh meat is the single food known to mankind that contains every one of the nutritional ingredients necessary for good health. It is entirely possible for man to live on meat alone. No particular parts need be eaten. Fat juicy sirloins, if that is what you prefer, will supply you with all the food necessary for top robustness even if you eat nothing else whatsoever for a week, a month, or a decade.

Each animal in the far and near places of this continent, every fish that swims in our lakes and rivers and streams, and each bird that inhabits the air is good to eat. Not only that, but nearly every part of North American animals is edible, even to the somewhat bland antlers that are not half bad roasted when in velvet and to the bitterish gall that has an occasional use as seasoning. The only exception is the liver of the polar bear, and of the ringed and bearded seal, which becomes so rich in Vitamin A at certain times that it is usually as well avoided.

Juicy fricassees, succulent stews, and sizzling roasts are fine fare. If anything, most of us would be happy eating more of this ideal grub which contains all the vitamins, minerals, and other nutriments necessary for full vigor. One way to accomplish this? By not passing up the birds and small game which are freely available to many of us through-out the entire year and which if not eaten will only be wasted.

GROUSE. Smoky fall days when you collect several young grouse or such from a covey, a worthy way to prepare them is by frying. Birds so cooked should be tender enough so that there will be no excuse to parboil them first.

90

Neither should they be encased in a thick shell of batter, nor kept soggy beneath a lid.

Disjoint the birds. Dip the sections in milk. Roll very sparingly in flour, salt, and pepper. If you've any thyme, try adding ⅛ teaspoon of that.

Get about 4 tablespoons of bacon drippings, bear fat, margarine, or the like sputtering in a heavy frypan large enough to hold all the pieces. Put the chunks in with the skin toward the bottom. Move to a cooler part of the stove and cook slowly, uncovered, until the uppermost meat is golden brown.

Turn the pieces just once. Cook another 15 or 20 minutes or however long it takes to make the skin tan and crisp. Then lay the chunks on a paper that will absorb the excess grease. Keep them warm while you ready the gravy.

For the gravy, leave only enough grease in the frypan to cover the bottom. Stir in 2 tablespoons of flour until thoroughly blended. Then very gradually add 2 cups of milk, along with ½ teaspoon salt, ⅛ teaspoon pepper, and ⅛ teaspoon paprika. Cook slowly, short of boiling, for 15 minutes, adding milk if thinning becomes necessary.

UPLAND FOWL. The trouble many cooks have in cooking some of the upland game birds stems from the fact that woodcock, quail, pheasant, and the like tend to run on the lean side. For half a dozen woodcock or quail, or an equivalent bulk of quartered pheasant, try:

> ¼ cup margarine
> ¼ teaspoon thyme (optional)
> ¼ cup chopped onion
> 1 teaspoon dried parsley
> 1 cup apple juice
> 1 teaspoon salt
> ⅛ teaspoon paprika (optional)
> flour

Spread open the small birds, cutting along the backbone and removing the nearly meatless bony parts. Quarter the pheasant. Roll sparingly in flour.

Melt the margarine or other fat in a heavy frypan. When

it is hot, brown the fowl. Sprinkle on the thyme. Cover and cook over low heat for 10 minutes.

Mix the chopped onion, dried parsley, and cup of juice which may be from cooked dried apples. Cover and keep simmering an hour or until done. About 10 minutes before the cooking is finished, sprinkle on the salt and paprika. A good accompaniment is rice—wild rice, by all means, if you can gather this expensive seed in your neck of the woods.

CREAMED GAME BIRD. Cut into strips or cubes the cooked meat of any leftover partridge or similar game bird. For every cup of meat, you'll want 2 tablespoons margarine, 2 tablespoons flour, ⅛ teaspoon salt, and 1 cup milk. A little powdered or plain dried celery will further enhance the flavor, as will a small amount of dried parsley.

Melt the fat in a heavy frypan. Stir in the seasoned flour until it is smoothly blended. Continuing to stir, gradually pour in the milk. Cook over low heat until creamy. Season to taste. Then put in the fowl and slowly cook until warm. Sprinkle lightly with dried parsley and serve.

TWO GAME BIRD SAUCES. In some regions, even when your major objective is big game, you can dine on ptarmigan, partridge, and other game birds about as often as you want. Here's a sauce that will afford a change of taste.

> 2 tablespoons margarine
> 1 medium-size chopped onion
> 1 tablespoon flour
> 1 can evaporated milk
> 1 tablespoon vinegar
> salt and pepper to taste

Melt the fat and fry the onions at low heat, turning them constantly and not allowing them to brown. When the onions are tender, gradually stir in the flour. Then add milk and vinegar. Bring to a boil and allow to simmer 15 minutes, stirring frequently. Season. This sauce goes well with all upland fowl.

When gunning is so good that you have a quantity of breasts to cook separately, mix:

½ cup cooking oil
1 cup vinegar
2½ tablespoons salt
1½ teaspoons poultry seasoning
¼ teaspoon pepper
1 minced clove of garlic

Bring these to a simmer. Then set off the stove and permit to cool. Soak the breasts in this sauce for an hour. Then broil or roast them until tender, basting with the remaining sauce. See if this one doesn't prove to all doubters that grub can be a pleasure as well as a necessity.

ROASTED WILD DUCK. Early season duck that are still in the pinfeather stage, duck that are to be stored frozen, badly shot birds, and those with fishy and other strong odors in the fatty tissue just beneath the skin will be considerably choicer eating if skinned.

Wild duck ordinarily are not stuffed. However, chopped or sliced onions, stalks or leaves of celery, soaked prunes or dried apples, or a few juniper berries are frequently placed in the cavity.

Set the well wiped duck in an open roasting pan with the breasts uppermost. Roast up to 25 minutes or so, depending on the size, in a very hot oven. Baste about every 5 minutes by spooning the hot juices over the birds. Duck will be tastier, juicier, and tenderer if kept very definitely to the rare side. Season to taste with salt and pepper after cooking.

This recipe is good, too, for sand hill crane.

WILD GEESE SPUTTERING. Roast wild geese in a slow oven until well done, allowing 18 to 20 minutes per pound. If you'd care to try a dried apricot stuffing, I can recommend this one:

¼ cup chopped onion
½ cup margarine
3 cups cooked rice
1 tablespoon celery seed or powder
1 teaspoon dried parsley
2 cups chopped dried apricots
1 diced carrot

1 teaspoon allspice
½ teaspoon salt
⅛ teaspoon pepper

Saute the onion lightly and politely in the margarine, only until tender. Remove from the heat. Add the other ingredients. Mix them together with just a few stirs. Stuff the goose. Truss. Roast in a moderate oven.

Wild geese, unlike their less active domestic brethren, tend to be dry and need frequent basting. The bird will be ready for the table when legs are loose and skin is appetizingly bronzed. Gravy may be concocted with drippings and giblets.

GEESE, SENIOR VERSIONS. Sometimes it is the older and less agile members of the flock that are bagged, whereupon the dutch oven may be called for.

Stuff the honker with equal amounts of well-soaked prunes and apple along with an onion to lend authority. Crisscross it with strips of bacon or salt pork. Set it in the heavy pot on a nest of carrots, potatoes, onions, parsnips, and any similar vegetables. Add hot water, with a chicken bouillon cube dissolved in each cup of fluid, until the fowl is about ⅓ covered. Put on the lid and cook very slowly atop the heat, or in a slow oven, until tender.

MALLARD. "My method of preparing this supreme wild fare is fairly simple," says Duncan Hines. "After washing and drying the duck, put a whole onion, a tablespoon vinegar, and a stalk of celery cut into long pieces inside it. Then set in a covered pan in a cold place overnight. This is for the purpose of eliminating all fishy flavor. These contents should be removed and discarded the next day.

"A sliced apple and a cut stalk of celery go inside the mallard next, but these, too, are discarded after the roasting. Lay 2 slices of salt pork diagonally across the breast of the duck. Put ½ cup olive oil and 3 tablespoons butter into a small roaster, and be certain it is very hot before putting in the duck. Roast in a hot oven for 15 to 20 minutes, basting every 4 to 5 minutes. My favorite accompaniment is wild rice and cranberry sauce."

QUAIL. Here is another savory and mouthwatering

delicacy passed along to me by Duncan Hines. Dredge 6 quail lightly in 1 tablespoon of flour, salted and peppered to taste. Now heat ½ cup butter and a tablespoon lard as much as possible without scorching. Add the birds and, turning them, brown fast to seal in the juices.

Then lower the temperature, add a cup of boiling water to the birds, cover the pan, and cook until tender. Add water as needed until you are ready to brown the breasts. After the water is gone, place the quail breasts down in the butter and brown over low heat.

For the gravy, remove the birds and stir a tablespoon of flour into the butter and juices. Add 1 to 1¼ cups of water to the flour mixture and scrape all the brown coating off the roaster into the gravy. Stir and cook until quite thick.

GIBLETS. These are just about the best part of any fowl, for my money. Clean the gizzards by carefully cutting to the hard center, then pulling this sac away from the meat with the fingers. Gently separate the bitter gall bladder from the liver, cutting out any part of the liver that is left with a greenish tinge.

Here's a good dish for sometime when you have a lot of these giblets; enough, say, for a couple of hearty eaters. Place the hearts and sliced gizzards into enough cold water, with ½ teaspoon of salt, so that you'll end up with 2 cups of broth. Adding feet and necks will give you a richer broth. Simmer for about 2 hours or until the hearts and gizzards are tender. Put in the livers the last 5 minutes of cooking.

Now get 2 tablespoons margarine or other fat melting in a frypan. Gradually add 2 tablespoons flour, stirring until it is smooth and thick. Saute ½ cup onion and ½ cup celery over low heat until tender. Then add the 2 cups of broth and get everything hot.

The hearts, gizzards, and liver go in next. Stir everything together over the low heat. If you want the gravy a little thinner or a little whiter, add evaporated milk. Salt and pepper to taste. Top with paprika and powdered parsley if you happen to have any.

All giblets taste pretty much the same. So, during off

seasons back in town, you may like to buy frozen chicken hearts so that you can repeat this repast often.

MUD HEN, ETC. Are men the best cooks? The Hudson's Bay Company says so. In its cooking course, prepared for the bachelor managers among its some 200 far-flung fur trading posts, the *Governor and Company of Adventurers of England trading into Hudson's Bay* state unequivocally, "The best cooks in the world are men."

My wife Vena suspects that this statement may be inserted largely as a morale builder, because a few sentences further along the potential "world's finest chef" is cautioned not to use his dishcloth to wipe off the stove. Yet the majority of good cooks in the North, certainly, are male. Some visiting sportsmen never do recover completely from the spectacle of hairy-armed sourdoughs lounging about a fur press and swapping recipes.

These old-timers go in mostly for plain cooking, although occasionally you'll meet a bannock puncher with a flair for the exceptional. One of these was rotund Ted Boynton, famous for more than a quarter century as one of the best trail cooks in the continental Northwest.

Whenever I see someone discarding some less favored waterfowl because they're "too fishy" or "too gamy," I remember how Ted Boynton used to handle birds of this sort. It's too bad, for several reasons, that more hunters don't know about it. Anyway, I guess one party figured they had Ted stopped the day they lugged in a brace of mud hen. One sportsman allowed as how he'd tried mud hen before. He said that if the part he got went over the fence last, somebody must have given it a boost.

Maybe it was the odors sifting into the atmosphere from the direction of Ted Boynton's fire. Maybe it was just curiosity, for a mud hen, although kind to its family and all, is generally about as tender and tasty as a discarded moccasin. At any rate, there was no second call that evening to the pan-banging accompanied, "Come and get it." There these fowl were, browned and bulging, looking as handsome as canvasback and smelling no less tempting than fat ptarmigan. Someone stuck his fork gingerly into a drumstick.

Moist steaming meat fell invitingly away from the bone. Everyone dug in hungrily.

"Even a loon don't cook up too bad," Ted told us, and later proved it, "if a yahoo don't try to gentle it aitch-for-leather. So don't throw mud hens or other such critters away, particularly in times like these. Cram them with onions. B'il real easy for three hours. Then start brand new with a crumb stuffing. Tuck a mess of sow belly or bacon strips where they'll do the most good. And roast nice and quiet like until a hungry man can't wait no longer."

PIGEON AND DOVE. The meat is dark of color and fine of flavor, that of pigeon having a tendency to be tough. Both are best cooked, tightly covered, in a small amount of water or tomato juice at low temperatures, either atop the heat or in the oven or reflector baker. Brown the birds first in a bit of cooking oil. Season with salt, pepper, celery or parsley flakes, and a small amount of chopped onion. Simmer usually from 30 to 45 minutes or until just tender.

CROW. Just as muskrat is more successfully merchandised as musquash and swamp rabbit, crow finds more takers when sold as rook. However, the dark meat is well worth cooking under any name. Tasting like chicken with appetizing overtones of duck, young crow is excellent either broiled or sauteed. Older varieties respond better to fricasseeing. If you've too many for friends and deep-freeze, then concentrate on the breasts.

H.B.C. PASTIES. Some of the best eating you'll find in northern Canada is at the Hudson's Bay Company trading posts. The following flexible recipe, geared in this instance to 4 partridge, is one of the reasons.

You'll also need 1 cup of raw potato and 2 tablespoons onion. Chop and mix these and the meat thoroughly. Salt and pepper to taste.

Now roll and cut some pastry dough into rectangles, about ¼ inch thick. Moisten the edges. Put generous portions of the meat mixture on one half. Then fold over the other half and seal the edges of the pastry well. Prick with a fork to make an escape vent for steam. Place on a pan and bake in moderate oven or reflector baker ¾ hour or until done. If any last that long, these are also memorable cold.

WILD TURKEY. It's hard to realize that back during early colonial years wild turkey was far more familiar to handhewn American tables than was domestic poultry. Remove the craw at once, or you are in for a disappointment. Matter of fact, the bird should be drawn as soon as you shoot it to make sure that it won't become too strong. This feast is worth all the personal attention you can give it. Cook by your favorite domestic turkey recipe.

BLUE GROUSE. The subtly flavored white meat of one of these big, plump fellows is just about the best you're going to sit down to in the game bird realm. Way I like them is cut into serving pieces, well rubbed with cooking oil, liberally salted, dusted with a few flakes of pepper, and then slowly broiled over hot coals. Start with the bony side toward the heat. Turn after about 10 minutes, again basting and seasoning. When a fork slips in easily and there's no gushing of red juices, the grouse is done.

You sometimes get a coat full of blue grouse, though, in high windy country where there's no satisfactory hardwood for coals. One way around is to use just the legs and breasts, saving the giblets and the rest for soup. Dredge the legs and breasts in salted and peppered flour. Now bring 6 slices of bacon slowly to a sputter in a heavy frypan. Remove the bacon to a hot dish when it is crisp. Quickly brown the grouse on both sides in the hot fat. Salt and pepper it, then remove to more moderate heat. Cover and cook 15 minutes, turning at about the halfway point.

Put the grouse on the hot dish with the bacon. Stir 2 tablespoons of flour into the fat and juice. Still stirring, slowly add 1½ cups of rich milk. When this has thickened the way you like it, season it to taste. Let each banqueter spoon his share over grouse, bacon, and any vegetables. With one ridge after another lifting in front of the late northern sun as you eat, and a breeze starting to trumpet a cool blue note, this is grub you're never going to forget.

LYNX. Lynx meat, served up to hearty appetites alongside a campfire, is except for fiber almost indistinguishable from the white meat of chicken. Because the larger lynx in particular are apt to be somewhat stringy, we like to cut the meat into very small pieces and fricassee these.

This you can do in a dutch oven if you want, preparing the meal before you leave camp in the morning and leaving it to reach a state of perfection by the time you get back ravenous at night. Or if someone is going to be in camp during the morning or afternoon, the meat can be trusted to cook slowly in a big kettle suspended over the fringes of the fire.

Start the meat as you would a stew in the bottom of a large receptacle. Allow it to simmer gently until tender. Such vegetables as onions, carrots, chopped celery, and in fact any you'd include with chicken go equally well with this dish.

You can make a gravy on the side if you want by blending 6 tablespoons of flour with a small amount of cold water, then adding 3 cups of the liquor from the pot and stirring until a thick sauce is the result. This may be poured over the lynx and vegetables. The fricassee goes well atop mashed potatoes, hot steaming bannock, or fresh fluffy rice. A little paprika will give it character. The flavor is surprisingly delicate. Unless so informed, no one would realize he was eating game.

BEAVER. One way to collect a heavily furred grizzly robe in the continental northwest is to accompany a trapper when he goes out in the spring for beaver. The great bear are so fond of fresh beaver meat that it's not unusual for them to raid a camp. When you've sat down to a feed of *amisk* after a day of making your way past steaming snow-drifts and seething streams, you'll better appreciate why.

Beaver meat is particularly rich. It's best, when possible, to stick to the tender youngsters. If you ever do cook up one of the big fellows weighing 40 to 50 pounds, a good thing to remember is that the meat will become more and more fibrous and stringy the longer it is cooked.

The ordinarily moist dark flesh is reminiscent, both in odor and flavor, of plump turkey. It is particularly excellent roasted, and when so cooked it has the advantage of not requiring any basting. For best results, trim off any excessive

fat first, and keep grease from accumulating in the pan. Cook in moderate heat. Cold, such meat is still moist and tasty in sandwiches.

"Noble creature," Dudley Shaw, Peace River neighbor, decreed once at lunch at my cabin, anchoring a slab of roast beaver between two slices of bread. "Glutted himself joyously with poplar."

"How can you tell?"

"*Amisks* who bog themselves down on willow," the old trapper explained, "are permeated with a bitterish flavor. And if they're crowded back into spruce, as happens on some congested ponds, the result is notoriously ghastly. Then the only thing you can do is parboil it copiously. Indians still scrape fat for a quick snack from even those hides, though. They roast the blinking stuff on green sticks propped by the fire while finishing skinning out the plunder. Cheers them up nobly."

BEAVER TAIL. Beaver tail was always something I very much wanted to try since reading, when a boy, Horace Kephart's regretful observation: "This tidbit of old-time trappers will be tasted by few of our generation, more's the pity." Because of wise conservation practices, the species has been making considerable of a comeback recent years, and, like you probably, I've had the pleasure of eating this delicacy on a number of different occasions.

Strung on a cord, as they're often carried, beaver tails look like nothing quite so much as scaly black fish whose heads have been removed. Heat causes the rough dark skin to puff and lift away, exposing a white and gelatinous meat. Somewhat resembling pork when boiled, this goes particularly well with such dishes as baked beans and thick pea soup.

PORCUPINE. "Many campers would pass up a porcupine, and yet he is one of the purest of all vegetarians. Again my memory goes back to when Bones Andrews, one of the last of the old mountain men of the breed of Jim Bridger, and I were compelled to spend several weeks in a region where there was no game. At the end of that time we had about the worst case of meat fever you can imagine. So we saddled up our little pack train and made tracks for higher altitudes and game country. On the way up I shot a porcupine. I skinned it, starting at the smooth underneath, and tied it to the back of my saddle.

"That night we made it into a stew. First, we cut it into small pieces and boiled these an hour. Then we added a handful of rice and salt, a dozen small dumplings of biscuit dough, and covered all that to boil 20 minutes longer. This was tall country. With air pressure lessening with the altitude, the higher you climb the longer you have to boil. We finally finished by adding a little flour to thicken the gravy and by stirring in a teaspoon of curry powder.

"Then the two of us sat down and finished the whole pot in one sitting. That pot held 9 quarts and was full. The quill pig, incidentally, should be a young one." (Colonel Townsend Whelen)

'POSSUM. The opossum's light colored and fine grained meat, all the tenderer because of mild flavored fat that's well distributed among the bands of lean, make it one of the most prized game animals in the southern states particularly. I prefer to skin them, at the same time removing the glands in the small of the back and inside the forelegs. The meat is better after it has aged a few days. If the 'possum is particularly plump, the answer as with bear is to cut off most of the outside fat and to keep grease from accumulating in the cooking pan. Salt and pepper. Roast in an oven or reflector baker.

'Possum is also exceptionally good when broiled over the open coals of the campfire. Cut it in half for this purpose. Or divide it into serving pieces. A small 'possum can then be individually cooked on forked sticks. If you want, baste it with your favorite barbecue sauce, although a lot of us would rather keep this latter for some less delicately flavored meat.

You can also brown 'possum in its own fat in the bottom of a dutch oven, season it with salt and pepper and perhaps ⅛ teaspoon of sage, add enough vegetables including sweet potatoes to go around, pour in 2 cups of hot water, and cook slowly until the meat is tender.

COON. The raccoon, one of the very cleanest of the game animals both in its eating and living habits, has dark, somewhat coarse, long fibered flesh whose flavor surpasses a lot of the veal and other meat for sale at the nearest market. Remove the kernel-like scent glands that are similar to the 'possum's. Trim off most of the exterior fat, and cook the same as 'possum. Roast coon, which takes 3 to 4 hours in a moderate oven, is famous. Coon is also excellent braised or broiled.

SQUIRREL. Squirrel, too, has little if any gaminess. The firm, lean meat needs added fat, but it can be advantageously cooked about every way. Lard it with bacon, season, and roast 1½ hours in a moderate oven. Or broil about a half hour or until tender, basting frequently. Or fry uncovered in a small amount of fat for from ½ to 1 hour, turning occasionally.

Or, particularly if the squirrel are the elders of their tribe, cut them up and roll each piece in flour. Brown slowly in a small amount of bacon drippings in a heavy frypan or dutch oven. Season with salt and pepper. Then add enough tomato juice or water to cover the bottom of the receptacle. Cover tightly and simmer in low heat from 1 to 1½ hours or until the meat is tender, turning it occasionally and if necessary adding enough liquid to maintain steam. Remove the cover the last 15 minutes for a crisper crust. Serve hot with gravy made by adding a small amount of water to the pan drippings, stirring it diligently over the heat, and seasoning to taste.

SQUIRREL STEW. If you only have a couple or so squirrel and some robust appetites to satisfy, the following stew may be the solution. Cut up the squirrel. Brown the pieces in the bottom of a pan in 3 tablespoons of margarine. Then cover with 3 cups water. Season only with 1 teaspoon salt and ⅛ teaspoon pepper so as to maintain the distinctive natural flavor. Simmer 1 hour.

Add ¼ cup chopped onion, ½ cup diced celery, and ½ cup sliced carrot. Thicken with a smooth paste made by blending 3 tablespoons flour with ¼ cup water. Cook an additional 15 minutes. If you want really to top this one off, roof it with dumplings made by one of the recipes suggested elsewhere.

ROAST MUSKRAT. Moist dark roast muskrat tastes like turkey, only better. The thing to remember is to remove the little glands under the hind and forelegs. Rub inside and out with an onion, and season all over with salt and pepper, using more pepper than you usually do.

If you want, fill loosely with a stuffing made in the proportions of 2 parts of soaked dehydrated apples and 1 part pitted and chopped cooked prunes. If you've any horseradish, include a teaspoonful of that.

Place the meat on a greased rack in a shallow pan. Brush generously with melted margarine or other fat. Lay several strips of bacon over the top. Roast in a moderate oven or reflector baker until tender, basting frequently.

Muskrat is also excellent both fricasseed and fried. For the former, make a well-seasoned brown gravy and simmer onions and pieces of muskrat in this until tender. Serve with rice. For the latter, disjoint the muskrat, parboil for 20 minutes if not young and tender, dip in flour, and fry in deep fat until golden brown.

WOODCHUCK. These are very much worth saving, particularly if after skinning you carefully remove the small glands from under the forelegs. Unless too grizzled and tough, they're generally best roasted. But if you run into a patriarch, brown the pieces in a small amount of fat. Then cover with water, season, and simmer 2 hours or so until tender. For a stew, add vegetables when the meat is nearly done. If any 'chuck is left over for serving cold, it'll be juicy and more flavorful if allowed to cool in the stock.

WILD GAME SOUP. This recipe is another from the Hudson's Bay Company. It calls for cutting up a rabbit or ptarmigan, although any similar game is also satisfactory. Put in a pot and simmer slowly for 2 hours with some left over vegetables, either 1 onion or 1½ tablespoons onion flakes, ¼ cup rice, 4 cups cold water, and salt and pepper to taste.

BRUNSWICK STEW. This huntsman's stew has been famous for centuries, so the recipes vary. The following is a good one, particularly when a day outdoors has whetted everyone's appetite. For four servings, disjoint a large rabbit or several squirrel or partridge so as to come by about 2 pounds of meat. Brown this in 2 tablespoons of fat in a heavy pot or frypan, along with ¼ cup of diced onions.

Add 1 cup tomatoes, 1 cup boiling water, and ⅛ teaspoon pepper. Cover and simmer until the meat is tender. Then put in 1½ cups lima or other green beans and 1½ cups of corn. Simmer 10 minutes or, if the vegetables were raw, until everything is ready. Season to taste with salt.

PICKLED RABBIT STEW. "Would you like a Midwestern recipe for the foremost American game animal, some 50 million of which are brought to the pot annually? If you would enjoy hasenpfeffer, 'First catch your hare,' goes the old saying. Some say it should be, 'First case (dress) your hare.' Anyway, you start with a 3-to-5 pound rabbit. Here is a good recipe:

"Cut the rabbit into pieces. Place in a marinade of: 2 cups vinegar, 1 cup claret, 1 cup water, 1 sliced large onion, ½ teaspoon salt, ⅛ teaspoon pepper, 1 teaspoon mustard seed, 1 teaspoon crushed juniper berries, 8 whole cloves, and 6 bay leaves. Marinate 1 or 2 days, turning at least every 12 hours.

"Then dry the meat carefully and sprinkle with flour. Saute in ⅓ cup of either butter or salt pork until well browned on all sides. Drain, then place in a pot. Strain the marinade through a sieve, add ½ cup water, and pour over the pieces of rabbit. Bring to a boil, cover, and simmer over low heat for about 45 minutes. Additional salt and pepper may be added if desired. Serve on a platter with the gravy—thickened somewhat with flour if you want—poured over it. Traditionally, hasenpfeffer is served with dumplings." (Duncan Hines)

RABBIT. The mildly flavored, finely grained meat of the rabbit and hare can be cooked like chicken, which it resembles. First, remove the glands from under the forelegs. Rabbit is so lean that even if you had all of it you could eat, you'd still starve to death on it alone. Add fat, though, and it's both nutritious and delicious. Cook like fowl and like other small game.

Smothered rabbit is a way out when you run into some of the older animals. With 2 rabbit, you'll need:

1	teaspoon salt
⅛	teaspoon pepper
½	cup flour
¼	cup fat
½	cup diced onion
1	cup milk

Mix the flour, pepper, and salt. Roll the serving pieces in this and brown them with the fat in a frypan or dutch oven. Add the onion and milk. Cover and simmer slowly for about an hour or until tender. Then remove the meat. Stir enough flour into the remaining juices to make gravy. Pour this over the meat. Sprinkle on paprika if you have it. Garnish if possible with parsley, either fresh or powdered, or with watercress. Serve over potatoes, rice, or hot bannock.

RABBIT FRICASSEE. One hungry wet night up by Sherwood Lake in New Brunswick, when our tent was leaking so much that we pitched it under an old brush leanto, Old Bill MacDonald took a couple of small rabbit I'd managed to bag, clattered around some in the grub box of our canoe, and came up with a fricassee that pushed back the rain and the shadows. By the next morning the rain had turned to tracking snow, and we were soon paddling back toward his Seven Mile Lake camp with a heavy buck.

Old Bill cut those rabbit into serving pieces and rolled them awhile in flour, salt, and pepper. Then he got ½ cup of butter sizzling in the bottom of a big iron frypan and slowly browned the chunks, forking them around all the time. He then poured in 2 cups of hot water from the boiling kettle, covered the frypan, and shoved it to one end of the grate where enough birch coals were falling apart to keep it simmering merrily.

After about an hour, he tested a meaty slab with a fork, nodded, and then stirred in a large chopped onion and a small can of peas. It couldn't have taken any more than 15 minutes to whip together a steaming batch of baking powder biscuits. Our stainless steel plates were so hot by then that I remember we had to put on a glove apiece to handle them. Old Bill eased a couple of biscuits on each plate, saturated them with butter, and then spooned rabbit over them until I begged quits. There was still enough for the seconds, at that.

CHAPTER 6

BY HOOK AND BY COOK

FISH

The way you cook your fish may be determined to some extent by their fatness. Plumper varieties such as lake trout, salmon, and whitefish are best for baking, as in a reflector baker or dutch oven, and for broiling over the cherry-red coals of a campfire. Their fat content helps keep them from becoming too dry.

Leaner catches such as pike, bass, perch, and Arctic grayling are preferable for poaching and for steaming because they remain firmer. They can also be satisfactorily baked and grilled if frequently basted or if topped with a sauce.

All fish are eminently suitable for frying. As far as that goes, any fish may be satisfyingly cooked by any of the basic methods if allowances are made for the fat content.

The main thing is not to overcook the catch. To keep fish moist and tender, and to bring out its delicate flavor, cook only until the flesh is no longer translucent. Once the fish is easily flaked, it is done. The taste will be further enhanced if the fish is salted, inside and out, as much as an hour in advance of cooking.

Second thing to avoid? Never soak any fish before or after it is cleaned.

SPITTED FISH. Some time when you have a mess of small brook trout or such, let everyone roughly trim and peel his own green hardwood wand. Thread a slice of bacon on the wand and broil it over ruddy coals until translucent. Then place the opened and cleaned fish lengthwise over the bacon, fastening the fish by skewering it with sharpened twigs. Cook slowly over glowing embers. Repeat as long as fish and appetites hold out.

Large fish may also be spitted and roasted over hot coals.

107

They have a tendency to roll on the stick, however, and usually must be lashed to it with twine or old fishline. Unless the fish is fat, it will be the better for basting.

KITED FISH. Naturally fat salmon, being self-basting, really lend themselves to this way of cooking which was a favorite among the Indians of the Northwest. I have also found this method effective with the Atlantic salmon of such famous Eastern rivers as the Southwest Miramichi and the Grand Cascapedia.

Open a salmon along the belly and remove entrails, fins, head, tail, and finally the backbone. Take care not to sever the back skin. Select a long, sturdy hardwood sapling and with your knife carefully make a split in it about twice the length of the fish. Open the fish like a book and ease it into the split, so that the sapling will loan the fish a solid spine and will extend well beyond it on both ends. Wrap some twine or wire securely around the split end of the stick.

You now need to spread the fish open. This you can accomplish by working a half dozen or so wooden crosspieces through the split stick and against both sides of the fish. Tie the ends of each pair of these together to hold the fish flat. You'll end up with something resembling a crude kite.

Sharpen the solid end of the sapling and stick it in the ground, so that the fish angles over a campfire that has burned to glowering coals. If a little smoke is wisping from the hardwood embers, the flavor will be all the better. Turn the fish after it has cooked to umber crispiness on the skin side. And be prepared to go fishing again tomorrow, and the day following, and the day after that.

SAUTEED FISH. This is hard to beat when it comes to fillets and small fish. Open and clean these latter as soon as possible after catching, saving the livers, hearts, and any roe. Unless you object to them too strenuously, leave on the head and certainly the tail´ where, in that order, lies the sweetest meat. Keep dry, cool, and well ventilated.

Get the frypan just hot enough that the butter or margarine in it barely begins to brown. You can roll the fish in flour, crumbs, or corn meal if you want, although I much prefer the rich crispy skin when it is unadorned. Brown on both sides only until the flesh flakes easily. The heart, liver, and any roe will then also be well done and tender. Transfer to a hot plate, unless you're eating alone maybe, and add any desired salt. If near civilization where such supplements are available, you may also like to squeeze on a few drops of lemon juice.

FRIED FISH. Dip the fillets, steaks, or the cleaned but otherwise whole pan fish into evaporated milk. For a richer crust, immerse next in beaten eggs. Roll finally in cracker, bannock, or bread crumbs. This will seal the flavor in and the cooking fat out.

Get this latter ½ inch deep and thoroughly hot, just short of smoking, in a heavy frypan, so that a protective coating will be quickly formed on the fish. Do not let the fat get any warmer, as this will cause both dryness and loss of flavor. Turn each piece of fish once. Although the cooking time will depend on the thickness of the catch, keep it on the under side if anything. When the fish flakes easily with a fork, it's ready for eating.

Fish so prepared can also be cooked in a hot reflector baker. Once they have been rolled in crumbs, place them in a warm greased pan and either dot with butter or margarine or pour a small amount of oil over them. This cooking method will give you more time for other chores. In about a dozen minutes, depending on the fish and the fire, the flesh will flake easily and be ready for the table.

BAKED FISH. A reflector baker and a large fish make a winning combination. Cover the fish well with butter, margarine, or cooking oil. Place in the greased pan with the skin down. Bake in front of a rousing fire as you would bannock. Baste occasionally. Turn the pan end-for-end about halfway through. About the only thing to beware of is overcooking. Test for flakiness as usual with a fork or twig. Too, baked fish must be fresh, or it will fall to pieces.

The larger fish can also be stuffed and baked if you want. A bread filling is a favorite. For a 5-pound fish, come as close as you can to:

¼   cup chopped onion
¼   cup margarine
5   cups bread crumbs
1   teaspoon salt
⅛   teaspoon pepper
1½   teaspoons thyme or poultry seasoning
¼   cup water

Cook the onion in the margarine until tender. Mix with crumbs, salt, pepper, and seasoning. Then add the water. Fill the fish loosely so that it won't burst and close it with whittled skewers. Bake in a hot oven or reflector baker, basting frequently. This will take about 10 minutes a pound. The usual flaking test will indicate when done.

With leaner fish in particular, this bread stuffing may seem somewhat dry. If you want and have the raw materials, substitute sliced tomatoes for the crumbs and omit the thyme and poultry seasoning.

FISH H.B.C. Hudson's Bay Company fur trading personnel have a recipe for whitefish that's good with other varieties as well. Fillet a large whitefish and divide it into 6 portions. Put 2 cups milk in a large frypan. Add a thinly sliced, medium-sized onion. Heat to the bubbling point and add the fish. Simmer until flaky, which will take about 20 minutes.

Now mix 1 tablespoon cornstarch in ½ cup milk. Remove the fish from pan and add the cornstarch mixture to the remaining liquid. Stir until it thickens. Then remove from heat and add a small piece of butter. Pour the sauce over the fish and serve with dry toast.

GRILLED FISH. The smaller the fish, the hotter the grill should be. If the fish sticks or breaks when you attempt to turn it or to take it up, then odds are you didn't let the grill get hot enough to start with. Too, grease it well at the onset.

Either salt the inside and outside of the fish up to an hour before broiling, or sprinkle the inside with pepper and lemon juice just before it goes on the heat. Whole fish may be split or not, depending on your preferences and on the size. Even when the fish has a thick skin well cushioned with fat, basting will add to the flavor. Once the translucency of the flesh has clouded to opaqueness, the fish will be ready for serving.

PLANKED FISH. These days if you can't easily come by a clean, sweet hardwood plank several inches thick, you can use almost any handy slab, shake, or other piece of wood of suitable size by first sheathing the working side with aluminum foil. The wood should be slightly longer and wider than the split fish.

Nail or peg the opened and flattened fish to the plank with the skin side toward the back. Salt and pepper. Either spread it with butter or margarine or brush it with cooking oil. Lean near the fire, turning the plank now and then and occasionally basting. As soon as the fish is flaky, it is ready. The saltiness of melting butter touches up the taste. If you've enough to go around, serve each fish with its individual hot plate attached.

BAKING FISH IN CLAY. This really seals in the flavor, but you need the kind of fine sticky clay that makes good log cabin chinking. If it isn't already wet, work it with water until it reaches the consistency of a stiff dough. Then mold it about an inch thick completely over the whole fish. Bury in hot embers until you have what resembles a hard, hot block. Baking will take about 15 minutes per pound of fish. When you break open the shell, you'll find such externals as fins and scales embedded in it, leaving a steaming savory feast.

POACHED FISH. Use serving size portions. Place in a frypan. Barely cover with hot salted water, tomato juice, or milk. Add diced onions if you want. Cover and simmer for about 10 minutes or until the fish is flaky. Then remove the fish and thicken the remaining gravy by stirring in flour and margarine. Pour the hot sauce over the fish and serve.

When fish is so poached in salted water, an egg sauce is a particularly fitting accompaniment. Melt 2 tablespoons of margarine in a separate pan. Blend in 2 tablespoons flour. Gradually stir in 1 cup of milk and cook about 5 minutes or until the sauce is thick and smooth. Remove from the heat. Season with ½ teaspoon salt and a sprinkle of black pepper. A ¼ teaspoon of paprika and 1 teaspoon of dried parsley will add eye and taste appeal. Finish by stirring in 2 finely chopped, hard boiled eggs. This sauce can be richly made with dried milk and eggs.

Fish may also be cradled in cloth or cheesecloth, lowered into salted bubbling water, and simmered gently until done. This is an easy way to prepare for recipes demanding flaked cooked fish. It is also a satisfactory way to cook a large salmon, part of which is to be eaten cold.

FISH CAKES. Colonel Townsend Whelen taught me this way of making fish cakes. You'll need:

1	small onion, chopped fine
2	tablespoons shortening
1½	cups cooked fish
3	cups diced, boiled potatoes
½	teaspoon salt
¼	teaspoon black pepper
1	tablespoon dried egg
½	cup water

Fry the onion in a small amount of the shortening until soft. Then mix with fish, potatoes, and seasoning. Stir the egg in the water. Add this and the remainder of the shortening to the other ingredients. Form into small cakes ¾ inch thick and fry in a greased pan until brown.

Another way both the Colonel and I like fish cakes on occasion is in the proportions of:

1	cup cooked fish
2	cups mashed potatoes
2	eggs, fresh or reconstituted
3	tablespoons shortening
½	teaspoon salt
¼	teaspoon pepper

Mix the potatoes and fish. Then stir the other ingredients into the mixture. Form cakes as before and fry them slowly until you can't wait any longer.

FISH CHOWDER. You can prepare for this before leaving on your vacation by packing and sealing dehydrated equivalents of the following or similar ingredients, except for the bacon and fish, in a plastic bag. Or you can make a quart of it on the spot with:

    1   cup diced potatoes
    ½   cup diced carrots
    2   tablespoons diced bacon
    1   tablespoon chopped onion
    ½   cup dry milk
    1½ tablespoons flour
    2   cups liquid (that from cooked vegetables
        plus water or fluid milk)
    2   cups flaked cooked fish

Cook the potatoes and carrots until tender in just enough boiling water to cover. Drain and save liquid. Fry bacon until crisp, adding onion long enough to make it tender.

Add milk powder and flour to the liquid and beat until smooth. Cook over low heat, stirring constantly until slightly thickened. Then combine all ingredients and heat thoroughly.

FISH PIE. Don MacDougall's most popular dish when he cooked for a Canadian Government survey party in the neck of the wilderness where I was fishing the other summer was fish pie. This Don got going by fitting an uncooked pie crust into what he described as a "real deep" casserole. A layer of fresh boiled fish, shredded, came next, then ½ inch of boiled rice, another thickness of fish, and so on. Each layer was sprinkled with salt and nutmeg.

Don then made a white sauce by melting 2 tablespoons of butter in a saucepan, slowly blending 3 tablespoons of flour with this, and seasoning the whole to taste. Then, all the time stirring, he gradually added 2 cups of milk and brought the sauce to a simmer.

He finally took a fork, punched holes in the pie, and cascaded the white sauce into these. A sliced onion went on top, and the whole concoction disappeared into a moderate oven for an hour.

ROE. This is so relished in Alaska that a stratagem there at the time of the herring runs is to anchor hemlock limbs along the shore so that roe from the spawning fish will catch in the branches. This roe is drained, seasoned with salt and pepper, and sauteed in moderate heat until brown on both sides. Cooking time is about 12 minutes. Add lemon juice to butter that's been heated to a delicate brown and pour this over the hot roe.

You'll also find herring roe scrambled with eggs in the 49th State. For about ½ pound of roe, add 1 tablespoon vinegar and 1 teaspoon salt to 2 cups boiling water. Add the roe and simmer 15 minutes. Drain and remove membrane. Mash the roe. Combine with 6 eggs, 6 tablespoons thick milk, ½ teaspoon salt, and ⅛ teaspoon pepper. Scramble the mixture in 2 tablespoons margarine or other fat in a frypan over low heat. Garnish with parsley, water cress, or such and serve hot.

LING LIVER. This is what Vilhjalmur Stefansson, greatest of the recent explorers, has long considered the finest delicacy the North has to offer. I've eaten a lot of ling, too, caught within casting distance of our Hudson Hope, British Columbia, homesite on Canada's Peace River. It certainly would be difficult to contest Dr. Stefansson's contention. The way I like these delicately flavored livers best is lightly fried in butter or margarine and eaten at once as is.

If you catch a good mess of this freshwater codfish, which many scientists call living fossils, and want to serve up something special for company, get a couple of frypans going. In the first, fry the vitamin-rich livers very lightly as before. In the other, fry some diced onions in butter or margarine until they're soft but not brown. A volume of diced onions about half that of the livers is about right. When the onions are ready, put them in with the livers. Stir both together gently, not breaking the livers, and cook a minute or so longer. Serve over hot buttered toast.

SHELLFISH

If you'd like to enjoy a wonderfully lazy day in the sun, with the nearly certain promise of catching a delicious meal, shellfishing is hard to beat. Everyone is sure to get something—spiny lobsters, or scallops, or maybe abalone in their mother-of-pearl shells. And what's better eating? Matter of fact, some of the best fun of all can be gathering driftwood, putting on a big kettle of salt water, and doing your feasting right on the shore.

CRABS. It's perhaps the crabs that provide more good sport and fine dining than any other North American salt water delicacy. There are so many ways to catch these pugnacious individualists that no one should have much trouble in getting his share. Just a chunk of meat tied to a string will turn the trick. Crabs attracted to it will hold on so persistently that you can easily yank them, dripping, from the water. By moving quickly enough at low tide, you can also scoop crabs of all dimensions out of the shallows where they sometimes lurk by the hundreds in swaying sea grass. A night light will bring them, swimming like luminous ghosts, to within easy reach of a long-handled net.

Any rake, its sharp tines blunted by tape, will excite some of these crustaceans to combat if advanced slowly through grasses and seaweed. When they've clamped tight, just lift them out. Similarly blunted garden forks will also serve. Or you can just poke around with a stick, pinning the crab if necessary until you can flip it into the damp burlap bag or pail of brine you're carrying.

Crabs are plunged live into boiling salt water. After 20 minutes of seething, they're ready for breaking open and eating with melted butter. Or the cracked legs may be dipped into a mixture of egg and crumbs, then fried in butter until brown and delicious. How about when crabs are in the soft-shell stage? Leaving the delicate new shell undisturbed, just saute them in a little butter. Once you've finished devouring the first batch, odds are you'll be out looking for more.

CLAMS. Then there are the clams. Almost all our coastal waters are enriched with these, and at least half the fun is getting out to harvest them. Sandy beaches, salty mud flats, gravel-loaded reefs, bright headlands, and foggy bays all yield their savory treasures. These vary from tiny bean clams, which after storms can sometimes be picked up by the hundreds along Southern California beaches, to huge geoducks weighing a dozen pounds and more.

Some of these clams are dug with shovels, rakes, forks, hoes, and trowels. Others are felt by barefooted waders who then casually reach down and transfer them to a convenient bag or basket. There are even clams, such as the succulent rough piddock, that hollow out homes in rocks and are hunted with such unlikely tools as sledge hammers and chisels.

On many a beach, the technique is to stroll along and tap the hard packed sand ahead, all the time watching for tiny holes to appear. At this sign that a clam is on the move somewhere beneath, the idea is to begin instantly digging on the seaward side. Some experts scoop away only the hard top surface, then grope for the fleeing clam with their hands. With a lot of species, you have to move surprisingly fast.

If there's any way clams can be cooked more delectably than they have been for centuries at New England clam bakes, then a lot of us haven't discovered it yet. All you have to do is dig a pit on the beach, line it with rocks, and kindle a roaring fire within. When the burning driftwood has crumbled to hot coals, spread on fresh wet seaweed. The clams go in next. They are immediately covered with more soggy live kelp. Then come such old standbys as unhusked corn and potatoes in their jackets, and a final topping of more wet seaweed. A thick layer of sand seals in both the heat and the wonderfully fragrant steam.

After about an hour, if you can wait that long, the now dry seaweed is raked out. The food is gingerly extracted. And everyone begins making with hot melted butter. But if your appetite precludes even these relatively simple preparations, just lay your live clams on a piece of sheet metal under which driftwood is flaming in all its different colors. When the shells have opened, cut out the clams, dip them in butter, and wash them down with sips of their own shell-cupped juices.

CLAM CHOWDER. Clam chowder is widely acclaimed. A sound rule is to make it of equal volumes of shucked clams, peeled and diced potatoes, and milk. Other ingredients can include a diced onion and several strips of bacon or salt pork. Boil the potatoes 5 minutes. Fry the bacon or salt pork until crisp and then brown the onion with it. Put together in a dutch oven or large pot and cook just short of simmering until the potatoes are done. Let some melting butter or margarine spread over the top. Salt and pepper to taste.

STEAMED CLAMS. This one brings memories of some particularly congenial hours spent with good companions beside rousing fires. A good way to get ready for such sessions is by washing your clams well in several changes of water, then spreading them out in a big shallow pan. Barely cover them with cold water, with 1 cup of salt to every 3 gallons of water, and let them stand 3 or 4 hours to cleanse themselves. This process you can help along by sprinkling on a cup of corn meal. Then, before you use the clams, make sure each is still alive. Any with yawning shells that don't close when handled should be discarded.

Place the clams in a dutch oven or large kettle. Add ½ cup boiling water for every 4 quarts of clams. Put on a tight lid and allow to steam over the fire until the shells partially open. This usually takes about 15 minutes.

Set the pot in the middle of the table. Have dishes of melted butter ready. Ladle some of the steaming hot broth into individual cups. Then let everyone use his hands, opening the shells one by one, stripping off the membrane and the outside of the neck, swishing the clam a bit in the broth, then dipping it in the butter, and plopping it into the mouth. By being careful not to disturb the sediment in the bottom of the cups, you can intersperse the eating with frequent sips of the rich salty liquid.

CRAYFISH. These are found under rocks and logs and in the banks of most streams although, inasmuch as they scavenge mostly at night, they are not too often noticed except by gourmets like the raccoon. However, these fresh-water crawdads will cling to bait with the same avidity as crabs. Cook them whole in a small amount of boiling, salted water until the crayfish turns red. Then peel and eat as you would lobster or crab. Don't throw away the tasty stock that remains. Add some diced vegetables to it, season if necessary, and you'll have some memorable soup.

ABALONE. Abalone are prizes along the Pacific Coast.

Once you've pried these great mollusks from rocks at low tide, scoop them from their bright shells with the same large screwdrivers or tire irons, trim off the dark sections, slice into thin steaks, and pound until soft. Dip these steaks into beaten egg, then cracker crumbs, and fry about a minute on each side. Abalone's distinctively delicate flavor, many believe, is enhanced by lemon juice.

Abalone chowder, too, is unforgettable. You'll need:

4	slices diced bacon
6	slices pounded and diced abalone
1	large diced potato
1	finely chopped onion
1	small clove garlic, crushed
1½	cups hot water
1	teaspoon Worcestershire
3	cups hot milk
	salt and pepper to taste

Brown the bacon. Then drain all but 3 tablespoons of the drippings from the pan. Add the abalone, the raw potato and onion, and the garlic. Saute until well browned. Now add the water, cover the pan, and simmer until the potatoes are tender. Blend in the remaining ingredients. Ladle out piping hot.

OYSTERS. There are the savory bay scallops, the cockles, prawns, shrimp, the rock lobsters, and the picturesque and exciting conches. There are also the tasty mussels that in the United States and Canada are found inland as well as along the coast. And there are the oysters; some of them even attached to the roots of trees. No other waters anywhere in the world will give the family or individual more fun or finer eating.

It is the oysters that guarantee some of the best meals our open places can provide. Eat them live. Roast them like clams. Roll in eggs, milk, and seasoned crumbs, and then fry in hot fat about 2 minutes or until brown. Steam and serve in the shells with melted butter. Shuck, drain, sprinkle with seasoned and buttered bread crumbs, and broil on the half shell for 5 minutes. Simmer them into stew with salt and pepper, butter, and a quart of milk per pint of shellfish. Alternate them on a green wand with slices of bacon and cook over the coals of the campfire.

Or conjure up what's known as Angels on Horseback with:

    1   pint oysters
    12 slices bacon
    ½   teaspoon salt
    ⅛   teaspoon pepper
    2   teaspoons dried parsley

Drain the oysters. Lay each oyster on half a slice of bacon. Sprinkle with salt, pepper, and dried parsley. Loop the bacon around the oyster and fasten with a toothpick or whittled skewer. Arrange the oysters on a rack in a shallow pan and bake them in a hot oven or in the reflector baker before a leaping fire. Pick up by the toothpick or skewer and eat hot.

ET CETERA

FROG'S LEGS. "The one dish that has lingered longest in my memory," Colonel Townsend Whelen tells me, "was comprised of 6-inch brook trout with many frog's legs which two of us 12-year-old kids prepared alongside a brook in the north woods."

Frog's legs are not unlike chicken in texture and flavor. Both front and hind are edible. The smaller the frog, the tenderer and sweeter they are. Strip the skin off like a glove. Either grill over open coals or fry in butter or margarine over low heat for 5 to 10 minutes or until the meat comes away easily from the bones. For frying, they may first, if you want, be rolled in lightly salted and peppered flour or bread crumbs. If you prefer a crusty coating, dip them between rollings in egg diluted with an equal volume of cold water. You can often gather a little water cress nearby whose spiciness will help bring out the flavor.

TURTLES. My experience has been with snappers. Get it biting on a stick, steady it with a foot on the shell, and behead it with an ax. Cut off the claws. Then turn it over and cut the skin all the way around. Skin the hide down the legs to the feet which can then be easily disjointed. Now with the help of a sharp knife in the case of snappers, or with a saw or ax with varieties such as terrapins, cut through the substance connecting top and bottom shells and pry off the latter. The entrails can then be easily reached and discarded.

If the turtle is a small one in ratio to the appetites involved, simmer it in the shell until the meat has cooked free. But if you've more turtle than you can eat, settle for cutting out the four quarters. Brown the meat in margarine or other fat in a heavy frypan. Add several sliced onions and enough water to cover. Cover and simmer until the meat is tender. Fork this onto mounds of mashed potato, cover with gravy made by stirring enough flour with the pan juices to thicken them, and fall to.

EELS. I've caught and eaten eels while trout fishing in New England and the Maritime Provinces, and this elongated fish outdoes all normal expectations. I like them skinned, cut into 2-inch pieces, salted, and then browned on both sides in the frypan with several tablespoons of margarine or butter.

FISHERMAN'S REPRIEVE. "White man crazy," a friend of mine, Howard Cook the artist, says an Indian guide told him once. "Look at watch to see if hungry."

Here's a fish dish which boasts its own built-in alarm clock for arousing even the most sated appetites. Listen to its taste-tingling sizzlings, catch a whiff of its subtly imposing aromas, or on occasion even as much as a glance at its goldenly darkening deliciousness, and good intentions are rerouted in favor of better and more immediate ones.

As a matter of fact, this recipe is one I generally reserve until the tag end of a successful season when, although he may not admit it, even the most dedicated purist would just as soon sit down to something besides the ordinary run of poached fish, steamed fish, baked fish, broiled fish, and of course fried fish.

It's a particularly good creation for which to make your preparations before taking off on a fishing trip. Outdoorsmen readying for an angling holiday can mix the necessary components at home except for water with which to re-constitute eggs and cream.

The following recipe is geared to enough fish to feed a hungry foursome:

- 4 eggs
- 1 teaspoon allspice
- 1 finely chopped garlic clove
- 2 tablespoons thick cream
- salt
- pepper
- flour
- ⅛ pound margarine
- 1 teaspoon chopped parsley
- 1 lemon

If using fresh products, break the eggs into a dish. Add the allspice, garlic, and cream. Then rub salt and pepper in proportions of a teaspoon of salt to every ¼ teaspoon of pepper into the fillets and soak them in the well beaten mixture 5 minutes. Sprinkle with flour. Fry them in the margarine until flaky.

Remove the fish and place on a platter or preferably on individual preheated plates. Now add any of the unused margarine to that remaining in the pan, stir in the chopped parsley, and squeeze lemon juice over both. Pour over the hot fillets.

For the streamside version of this fish dish, substitute equivalent amounts of powdered whole eggs, parsley flakes, dehydrated cream, and dried lemon juice. Seal in a plastic bag with a hot iron or adhesive cellulose tape. When ready to use, add enough water to make a thick batter and proceed from there.

CHAPTER 7

BANNOCK, SOURDOUGH & OTHER BREADS

About the only cooking odors that even approach the aroma of bread baking outdoors are the sizzling smell of good grilled bacon, coffee bubbling in the heat of a campfire, and fat venison sputtering over hardwood coals.

This is just as well because, unless you can replenish it frequently, bakery bread soon becomes moldy, stale, and thoroughly unappetizing in the out-of-doors. Furthermore, its airy softness is unreasonably bulky and unsubstantial when it comes to packing. All these shortcomings are especially apparent when you consider that even the rankest greenhorn can break himself off a hot chunk of steaming bannock after a few minutes of practically foolproof effort.

Sourdough bread, too, is particularly designed to solve the problems of the ofttimes unskilled wilderness cook. Considerable folklore has sprung up around this pioneer staple which, early proving its ability to rise under just about any condition short of freezing, gave veteran northerners their name.

You hear tales of sourdough that has been kept going ever since gold rush days near the turn of the century. Many such accounts are completely true. The main difference between the folklore and the facts is one of cleanliness. There's actually no big need to worry about the admonition of old bushmen that if sourdough turns orange or yellow, it's still good; but that if it takes on a moldy greenish hue, it should be discarded and a new starter mixed.

When I first began log cabin living at Hudson Hope, British Columbia, I followed the practice of trapper neighbors and kept the sourdough starter in a surely handy lard pail. The difficulty was: the acids in sourdough corrode metals, discoloring and subtly changing the sponge. But more about that in a moment.

Another custom of the country I briefly adopted was that of keeping the sourdough working by dropping in leftover pancakes, crusts, and the like. This procedure, I discovered, adds nothing to the flavor while often worsening it considerably. Such haphazard additions, furthermore, are apt to keep you discarding spoiled starters and beginning new ones. More about that, too.

In other words, there are some good easy ways around the bread dilemma. Here are a few of these detours.

FRYING PAN BREAD. This is the famous bannock of the open places. The basic recipe for one hungry outdoorsman follows. If you want more, increase the ingredients proportionately.

> 1   cup flour
> 1   teaspoon baking powder
> ¼   teaspoon salt

Mix these dry, taking all the time you need to do this thoroughly. Have the hands floured and everything ready to go before you add liquid. If you are going to use the traditional frypan, make sure it is warm and greased.

Working quickly from now on, stir in enough cold water to make a firm dough. Shape this, with as little handling as possible, into a cake about an inch thick. If you like crust, leave a doughnutlike hole in the middle. Dust the loaf lightly with flour, so it will handle more easily.

Lay the bannock in the warm frypan. Hold it over the heat until a bottom crust forms, rotating the pan a little so the loaf will shift and not become stuck.

Once the dough has hardened enough to hold together, you can turn the bannock over. This, if you've practiced a bit and have the confidence to flip strongly enough, can be easily accomplished with a slight swing of the arm and snap of the wrist. Or you can use a spatula, supporting the loaf long enough to invert the frypan over it and then turning everything together.

With a campfire, however, it is often easier at this stage just to prop the frypan at a steep angle so that the bannock will get direct heat on top. When crust has formed all around, you may if you wish turn the bannock over and around a few times while it is baking to an appetizing brown.

When is the bannock done? After you've been cooking them awhile, you will be able to tap one and gauge this by the hollowness of the sound. Meanwhile, test by shoving in a straw or sliver. If any dough adheres, the loaf needs more heat. Cooking can be accomplished in about 15 minutes. If you have other duties around camp, twice that time a bit farther from the heat will allow the bannock to cook more evenly.

OTHER COOKING METHODS. Instead of slanting the pan in front of the fire to cook the top side only, you can often bake it throughout at this second stage. This may be accomplished by the use of an existing boulder or some such reflecting surface, perhaps several large stones laid up beside the campfire for the purpose. When the reflecting area is hot, lean the pan with its back to this and its face to the direct heat.

A reflector can also be made by thrusting several stakes in a line a foot behind the fire to support an expanse of aluminum foil. Or, with a small bannock, you can just bend a small sheet of foil in an arc over the frypan so that the heat rising about the pan will be reflected back down onto the top of the food.

You can also scoop a small pit in front of the campfire, rake a few red coals into it, and set the frypan on these so the bannock will be cooked both by the embers below and the blazing forelog of the fire above. For best results, this forelog should be a well burning one that's lying several inches off the ground at this point and blazing upwards with a generally vertical flame.

Suppose you're short on utensils and long on appetites? As soon as each loaf is crusty enough to hold its shape, slide it out of the pan and lean it on the ground near enough to the campfire to finish cooking. Immediately start another.

Bannock is also cooked with a minimum of attention in ovens of all kinds. This is a major reason for considering one of the folding wood stoves with ovens when traveling by car, boat, or horse. These stoves come in various models and sizes. The next handiest convenience, when you have the room for it, is a folding camp oven, preferably one with a heat indicator. Besides their uses with wood fires, these make baking with a manufactured-fuel stove—and, incidentally, with that charcoal grill when you get back home—a simplicity.

Bannock, in any event, never tastes better than when devoured piping hot around a campfire. It should then be broken apart, never cut. A cold bannock sliced in half, however, and made into a man-size sandwich with plenty of meat or other filler in between is the best lunch ever.

REFLECTOR BAKER. Light and compact varieties of the reflector baker, which our pioneer ancestors used for baking in front of open fireplaces, are still invaluable out-

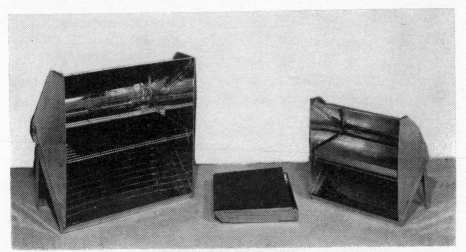

REFLECTOR BAKER.

door equipment. The modern articles are made of brightly reflecting metals such as aluminum. They fold flat for easier carrying. Because they operate on the principle of reflecting heat to all parts of the cooking food, maintenance of their efficiency depends on their being kept reasonably clean and bright.

These portable ovens provide the simplest and most convenient means of baking and roasting with an open fire. They are also used in conjunction with ovenless stoves. Not only breads and biscuits, but fish and game as well, come out hot and appetizing. You merely stand the reflector before a blazing fire or hot stove. The temperature you regulate by moving the contraption toward or away from the heat. Food is placed in a pan on the center shelf of the reflector oven and occasionally turned end for end so the baking will be more uniform.

Here is a fine way to cook bannock in loaf form. For instance, you want some handy slices between which to sandwich cold venison for the next day's lunch. Use the basic bannock recipe, probably in at least double proportions, but shape the dough into a loaf. Dust lightly with flour. Lay in a warm, greased pan. Place this in the oven. Bake with occasional turnings of the pan until you get a good looking crust and the testing sliver comes out without any dough adhering.

BISCUITS. Start with the basic bannock recipe. Work 3 tablespoons of solid shortening per cup of flour into these dry ingredients. Mix thoroughly, perhaps by cutting through the flour and shortening again and again with two dull knives, until the mixture has the consistency of coarse meal.

REFLECTOR BAKER USED WITH FOLDING STOVE.

Then, working quickly, add enough water or milk to make a dough just soft enough to be easily handled. From ¼ to ⅓ cup of fluid per cup of flour will generally suffice. If the dough becomes too sticky, rapidly scatter on a little more flour. For best results, knead no more than half a minute.

Flatten the dough speedily into a sheet about ¾ inch thick. A cold bottle or can makes an effective rolling pin. Cut square biscuits with a sharp cold knife or press out round ones with perhaps the top of the baking powder tin. Dust each with flour.

Place on a lightly greased pan or sheet. Bake in a very hot oven or reflector baker until a rich brown, by which time the biscuits should have risen to about 2 inches high. These biscuits can also be cooked in a frypan like bannock, in which case you may have to turn each one several times to assure even cooking. If you don't care for crust, keep them close together. Or bake them in a dutch oven, as suggested later in this chapter.

Want something special? Dip each biscuit into melted shortening before baking.

BAKING POWDERS. When liquid is added to baking powder, gas is released. This is the same harmless carbon dioxide that gives such beverages as ginger ale their bubbliness. Its function in breadstuffs is to raise the dough. Without some such effervescence you'd end up with a chunk of hardtack; the way to make this, incidentally.

It follows that you want to prevent as much as possible of this gas from wastefully escaping. Aside from speed, you can conserve it several ways. Cold fluid, as might be expected, releases the carbon dioxide more slowly than hot. It is also better to do as much of the necessary mixing as possible with a cold spoon or peeled stick rather than with the warm hands.

Why not just put in more baking powder? The answer is that food tastes better and digests more easily with a minimum of this acid-alkali combination. Some outdoor cooks do tend to take out insurance by using more than the teaspoon of baking powder that's generally sufficient for each cup of flour. It's true that strengths of this leavening agent vary. Furthermore, all baking powder tends to become weaker with age, particularly if the container has not been kept tightly closed and in a dry and preferably cool place. It's sound practice to stir baking powder a bit before measuring, partly to break up any lumps but mainly to assure a more uniform mixture of ingredients. The outer layer is apt to lose some of its leavening power because of contact with air.

Directions on the particular can if the contents are fresh, experimentation if they are not, will provide a functional yardstick if you've any doubts. Double action baking powder, the so-called combination type which releases part of its gas when heated, packs more power than either the tartrate or the calcium phosphate varieties. The recipes in this book are geared to it.

The ideal, insofar as flavor and digestion are concerned, is to use the smallest amount of baking powder that will raise the breadstuff enough for your liking.

How to find out if the baking powder in your camping outfit is still active? Stir a teaspoonful into ½ cup of hot water. If the mixture doesn't bubble diligently, better use sourdough instead.

MIXING THE DOUGH. Easiest and most economical way is to carry a small sheet of thin plastic. Bark may also be used, but at best it's a nuisance. Wax paper or foil is an answer for motorized campers.

Prospectors, trappers, and other professional outdoorsmen still widely continue the pioneer practice of mixing bannock in the flour sacks themselves. Just make a small hollow in the flour. Drop the salt and baking powder into this. Then, stirring with the fingers of one hand, add the water gradually until the resulting dough has picked up all the flour it needs. Press and pat into shape. Cook.

BANNOCK CHANGES. Variations on the basic bannock recipe are innumerable. Inclusion of a tablespoon of sugar with every cup of flour will make for a more pronounced taste and a crisper crust. Fresh or powdered eggs, ½ to 1 egg for every cup of flour, will add thickness and richness.

Substitution of milk for water, or the addition of powdered milk, will improve both flavor and characteristic golden brownness.

Addition of a shortening, usually from 1 to 3 tablespoons per cup of flour, will increase tenderness. This is especially desirable in winter sports weather when even larger proportions of fat are sometimes necessary to keep the breadstuff from freezing hard on frosty trails. Solids like butter, margarine, bacon drippings, and lard are most effective when either creamed with the sugar or thoroughly mixed with the flour. Liquids such as cooking and salad oils, which make for a more crumbly but not so tender product, may be added mixed with water, milk, and any fresh eggs.

Such fruits as raisins, currants, and blueberries make bannock tastier, although their inclusion calls for the use of a bit more baking powder. Combine these fruits with the dry ingredients to avoid any overmixing. Spices, particularly nutmeg and cinnamon, are unusually zestful when their odors mingle with the keenness of pine trees and wood smoke.

MAPLE MUFFINS. You don't need maple trees for these. If you want, just make up some of the substitute maple syrup described elsewhere in this book. Then take:

- 2 eggs
- ⅓ cup milk
- ½ cup syrup
- 4 tablespoons liquid shortening
- 2 cups flour
- 2 teaspoons baking powder
- ¼ teaspoon salt

Add the eggs, either whole or dried, to the milk and beat together. Mix the syrup and shortening. Stir this into the eggs and milk.

Combine the flour, baking powder, and salt. Add the rest, mixing just enough to moisten the dry ingredients. Pour into a greased muffin pan and bake in a moderate oven or reflector baker. About ½ hour should do it. If these muffins are not devoured on the spot, loosen them in the pan, tip them so that air can get around them, and put them in a warm place.

SNOW FOR EGGS. In the North when we have lacked eggs for this and other breadstuffs, we have successfully used snow instead. Fresh dry snow is best for this purpose. It is rapidly stirred in just before the breadstuff is put over the heat. It must not be allowed to melt until the cooking is underway, for its function is entirely mechanical.

The air-loaded flakes of snow hold the ingredients apart. Cooked while these are so separated, such breadstuffs come out airy and light. Egg is able to accomplish the same end result, as you can appreciate by watching the way an egg readily beats into air-holding froth whose elasticity heightens its raising and spacing prowess. Two heaping tablespoons of fresh dry snow will take the place of every egg in the batter.

HOMEMADE DRY MIX

Fresh bannock is a simple thing to cook on the trail, even when the nearest utensil is a dozen miles away. Then the handiest method is to mix the dry ingredients before leaving the base of supplies. In fact, you can make up a number of such batches at home, sealing each in a small plastic bag. This mix has multiple short-notice uses.

The following basic mix, given here in one-man proportions, will stay fresh for six weeks or more in camp if kept sealed, dry, and reasonably cool.

- 1 cup all-purpose flour
- 1 teaspoon double action baking powder
- ¼ teaspoon salt
- 3 tablespoons oleomargine

If this mix is being readied at home, sift the flour before measuring it. Then sift together the flour, baking powder, and salt. Cut in the margarine with two knives, with an electric mixer at low speed, or with a pastry blender, until the mixture resembles coarse meal. For increased food value, add 2 tablespoons of powdered skim milk for every cup of flour.

Place in plastic bags. Seal with a hot iron or with one of the plastic tapes. A large quantity can be made at once, of course, and divided into smaller portions. Before using, it is a good idea to stir the mixture lightly.

If compounding this mix in camp, do it with the ingredients at hand and in the simplest way possible. Any solid shortening may be utilized if the mix is to be used within a short time. Such mix may be carried in a glass jar or just folded in wax paper.

DRY MIX PRODUCTS

FOR HOT TRAIL BREAD. When the fire is going and everything else is ready, quickly add enough water to basic mix to make a firm dough. Shape into a long, thin roll, no more than an inch thick. Wind this ribbon on a preheated green hardwood stick, the diameter of a rake handle, so trimmed that several projecting stubs of branches will keep the dough in place. A particularly sweet wood for the job is birch. Hold the bannock in the heat, occasionally turning it, for a couple of minutes. Once a crust has been formed, the stick may be leaned between the fringes of the fire and some reflecting surface such as a log or rock for the 15 minutes or so required to form a tasty brown spiral. Or you can just shove a sharpened end of the stick into the ground beside the fire and turn this holder now and then while readying the remainder of the meal.

FOR FRYING PAN BREAD. When ready to go, add to mix about ⅓ cup of cold water for an easily handled dough. Cook like regular bannock.

FOR DROP BISCUITS. Mix with a little less than ½ cup cold water to make a soft dough. Drop by the spoonful atop a hot greased metal surface and bake in a very hot oven or reflector baker for 10 to 15 minutes.

FOR FRUIT COBBLERS. Proceed as with the above biscuits, but drop each daub of dough atop a frying section of apple, apricot, or other cooked dry fruit.

FOR MUFFINS. Add 1 tablespoon sugar, 1 well beaten whole or reconstituted egg, and ½ cup milk. Stir just enough to dampen all the dry ingredients. Fill greased muffin rings, improvised if necessary from aluminum foil, about ⅔ full. Bake in a hot oven about 20 minutes. Eat at once. For a dessert, cook with a teaspoon of marmalade or jam atop each muffin.

FOR SHORTCAKE. Add 1 tablespoon of sugar to make half a dozen medium-size shortcakes, which will assure a pleasant change of diet in berry season. Mix with ⅓ cup cold water to form an easily handled dough. Flatten this to ¼ inch and either cut squares with a knife or punch out ovals with something like a can top. Brush half of these with melted margarine. Cover each with one of the remaining pieces. Bake in reflector baker. Serve hot with fruit.

FOR CORN BREAD. Add a previously mixed 1 cup corn meal, 1 tablespoon sugar, 1 beaten egg, and 1 cup milk, stirring only until blended. Bake in hot oven or reflector baker about half an hour. Corn bread, like biscuits and baked potatoes, should be served as promptly as possible.

FOR FLAPJACKS. Add ½ cup milk, with which a whole or dried egg has been mixed, to the homemade dry mix. Stir only enough to moisten the flour. Cook like regular flapjacks.

FOR DUMPLINGS. Stir in ¼ cup of cold milk or water. Proceed as with regular dumplings. These can also be dropped by the tablespoonful atop a meat or vegetable casserole and baked in a hot oven approximately 20 minutes.

FOR COFFEE CAKE. Stir 3 tablespoons sugar into the mix. Combine a scant ¼ cup milk with 1 egg, fresh or dried, and stir well into the mix. Pour into shallow greased pan. Sprinkle something such as nutmeg, cinnamon, powdered instant coffee, and sugar over the top if you want. Bake in a hot oven or reflector baker about 25 minutes. Delicious!

SOURDOUGH

Sourdough was the first raising agent ever used in bread making. The primitive leaven contained wild yeasts as well as numerous kinds and types of bacteria, some of which produce gas and acids. If desirable organisms were to gain supremacy, the leaven was a success. If the fermentation was dominated by undesirable organisms, the product was inferior. Knowing all this, we can now control our sourdough to a large extent.

You can still make a primitive sourdough starter by mixing a cup apiece of plain flour and water in a scalded jar, covering it loosely, and placing it in a warm place to sour. If the first results are not satisfactory, you may try again with a new mixture. Trouble is, you run into all sorts of different flavors and consistencies. If you will enlist the help of store yeast, however, you can almost always come up with a satisfactory starter of your own on the first try.

SOURDOUGH STARTER. The starter can be readied at home. Once you have it, you have commenced growing your own yeast. That's what you are actually using when you bake with sourdough. Here's the sure, simple way to begin:

> 2 cups flour
> 2 cups lukewarm water
> 1 yeast cake or package of dry yeast

Mix the flour, lukewarm water, and yeast thoroughly. Then set overnight away from drafts in a warm place. By the next morning, the mixture should be putting forth bubbles and a pleasant yeasty odor. This over-all process needn't stop for as long as you're going to be in the wilderness.

For best results, keep the starter in a well washed and scalded glass or pottery container. Never leave any metal in contact with it. Keep the starter as much as possible in a cool spot. As a matter of fact, if you want to store the starter or part of it for a period of months, just freeze it.

The sourdough starter can also be kept fresh and clean by drying. If you want to carry it easily and safely, work in enough flour to solidify the sponge into a dry wad. A good place to pack this is in the flour itself. Water and warmth will later reactivate the yeast plants for you.

Starters occasionally lose their vigor, particularly in cold weather. Old-timers then sometimes revive them with a tablespoon of unpasteurized cider vinegar. This puts new acetic acid bacteria on the job. A tablespoon or two of raw sour milk or cream, of unpasteurized buttermilk, or of cultured buttermilk or cultured sour cream will get the lactic acids functioning again.

Sourdough starters should never be stored in a warm place for very long. Heat encourages organisms hurtful to yeast to grow at an extremely rapid rate. These may soon gain sufficient control to produce putrefactive changes; the reason for some of the unpleasant smells one occasionally runs across in old starters. Another result is that the starter becomes progressively weaker in dough-fermenting ability.

The sometimes necessary solution? Begin a new starter. This is a practical reason for including some spare yeast in the camping outfit. Best to take is recently dated, packaged dry yeast. Stored where reasonably cool, this will keep several months or more.

A sourdough starter is best kept going by the addition of flour and water only. The starter, unless temporarily frozen or dried, should be so fed about once a week at least. If you are regularly cooking with the starter, this process will take care of itself.

SOURDOUGH BREAD. If commencing from the beginning, set your starting sponge as already directed. The commercial yeast is used only to get the starter going. From then on, the mixture will grow its own yeast. When doubling a recipe, by the way, you needn't double the starter.

Take your starter. Add enough flour and lukewarm water in equal volumes to make about 3 cups of sponge. Let this stand in a warm location overnight or from 6 to 8 hours, whereupon it should be bubbling and giving off an agreeable yeasty odor.

From here on, the general procedure remains the same. Take out, in this instance, 2 cups of sponge. Place the remainder aside. That's your next starter. No matter what the recipe, at this stage always keep out about a cup of the basic sourdough.

To these 2 cups of sponge add the following:

    4 cups flour
    2 tablespoons sugar
    1 teaspoon salt
    2 tablespoons shortening

Mix the flour, sugar, and salt. Make a depression in the center of these dry ingredients. Melt the shortening if it is not already liquid. Blend it and the sponge in the hollow. Then mix everything together. A soft dough should result. If necessary, add either flour or fluid. The latter may be water or milk. Knead for 3 or 4 minutes on any clean, floured surface.

"Keep attacking," I can still hear an old trapper cautioning, eyes blinking amiably behind thick-lensed spectacles. "Don't gentle it. That is where most cheechakos make their mistake. Too much pushing and pressing lets the gas escape that's needed to raise the stuff. Just bang the dough together in a hurry, cut off loaves to fit your greased pans, and put them in a warm place to raise."

The dough, once it has plumped out to double size, should be baked some 50 to 60 minutes in a moderately hot oven or reflector baker that, preferably, is hottest the first 15 minutes. Baking should redouble the size of the loaves. One tests "in the usual way," the old trapper added. He explained, probably because it seemed necessary, that the "usual way" is to wait until the loaves seem crisply brown, then to jab in a straw. If the bread is done, the straw will come out dry and at least as clean as it was when inserted.

Sourdough bread is substantial in comparison with the usual air-filled bakery loaf. It keeps moist for a satisfactorily long time. When the bread is made according to the preceding suggestions, the flavor is unusually excellent, being especially nutty when slices are toasted. If your crew likes real tasty crust, bake the bread in long slim loaves to capitalize on this outstanding characteristic.

BAKING IN THE GROUND. During the gold rush days at the turn of the century, when gravel punchers stampeded past my present Hudson Hope, British Columbia, homesite toward where dust lay yellower and more beckoning beneath the northern lights, prospectors used to bake sourdough bread in the shallow steel vessels used for panning gold. A few still do, for that matter.

A shallow hole was scooped in the ground, often in the heat-retaining sand of a stream bank. A fire was allowed to burn to coals in this cavity. Dough, in the meantime, was rising between two gold pans. Some of the ruddy embers were raked out of the hole. The pans were inserted and covered with the hot residue, plus maybe a few coals from the regular campfire. One hour's cooking in this makeshift oven was generally the minimum. The bread wouldn't ordinarily burn if allowed to remain longer. The crust would just thicken and become more golden, that's all.

You don't need gold pans to do this today. Other utensils, as for example two preferably large heavy frypans, will accomplish the same thing. If the metal is light, insulate it all around with a thin covering of ashes.

DUTCH OVEN. This highly effective oven of heavy cast iron, described in an earlier chapter, will bake biscuits and breads deliciously both below and above ground. Heat the contraption first, setting the lid on a good solid fire and easing the pot atop that. When the pot is hot, you should be all set to go.

Say you want to bake a mess of baking powder biscuits. Drop a blob of grease into the pot and work it around a bit. While it's melting, ready the biscuits. Put them in the pot

DUTCH OVEN.

and plant this solidly and evenly above a bed of coals and ashes. Clank on the lid. Heap additional coals onto that. The fact that the lid has been preheated to a higher temperature than the pot should balance the natural rising tendency of heat sufficiently to cook the tops and bottom of the biscuits uniformly.

Take a look after about 10 minutes. If the biscuits aren't already taking on a healthy tan, rake the accumulating cinders and ashes from the lid and substitute more live coals. Dutch ovens require a certain amount of cooking experience, but the biscuits should ordinarily be ready in a dozen or 15 minutes.

Bread, taking longer to bake, is better adapted to underground cooking. For this, start in the forenoon by digging a hole somewhat larger than the oven and filling it with a blazing hardwood fire. A basic precaution? Be sure this pit is in mineral soil, well away from roots and humus, so that the fire can not spread in any direction. When the blaze has burned down to coals, shovel out about half of them. Set in the preheated and greased dutch oven with a big round sourdough loaf bulging in it. Ease the oven around until it's setting evenly. Then rake the embers and ashes back in until the utensil, except for its upraised bail handle, is hidden.

You need a certain bit of experience here, too. If it seems that the coals are going to be too ardent, insulate the oven with an inch or so of ashes. In any event, seal in the heat with several inches of dirt. Then spend the afternoon getting enough trout or grouse to go with those crusty hot slices that will be awaiting you at suppertime.

BEATEN SOURDOUGH BREAD. This bread is especially popular with outdoorsmen cooking for themselves. One reason is that it's unnecessary to touch the dough with the hands, sometimes a particular boon as when you've been blazing a trail and your fingers are sticky with pine pitch.

Proceed as with regular sourdough bread. Instead of kneading the dough, however, beat it for two minutes. Then leave it standing in the mixing bowl until it has bubbled itself to lightness.

Add 1 teaspoon baking soda. Mix another minute. Then turn into a well greased container and let stand 10 minutes in a warm place. Bake in a moderately hot oven or reflector baker 50 to 60 minutes or until done.

SOURDOUGH FLIPPERS. A lot of fishermen, campers, and other frequenters of the farther places don't figure they've started the day right until they have stoked up with a stack of hot, tender, moist sourdough flapjacks. These flippers, as sourdoughs often call them, are so easy to prepare that there's no need for even the greenest tenderfoot to be dependent on store mixes. They're so tasty and wholesome, furthermore, that many a vacationist looks ardently for more when he's shut in again by city streets.

For a couple of breakfasters, add 2 cups flour and 2 cups lukewarm water to your sourdough starter. Set overnight away from drafts in a warm location. The next morning return the original amount of starter to its scalded glass or earthenware container. To the remaining batter add:

- 2 eggs, fresh or dried
- ½ teaspoon salt
- 1 tablespoon sugar
- 1 teaspoon soda
- 1 teaspoon warm water
- 2 tablespoons liquid shortening

Mix the eggs, salt, and sugar with a fork. Melt the baking soda in the teaspoon of warm water. Stir all these into the batter, along with either cooking or salad oil, or melted lard, margarine, etc.

For variations from time to time, if you ever want them, add a little whole wheat flour, corn meal, bran flakes, or such to batters after the starter has been saved out.

If the flapjack batter becomes a bit too thick to pour easily, thin it with just enough milk. Flour, on the other hand, will provide stiffening. But if the batter is on the thin side, the flippers will be more tender.

Once the preferably heavy frypan or griddle is hot, grease it sparingly with bacon rind. Do not let the metal reach smoking temperatures. Turn each flipper once only, when the hot cake starts showing small bubbles. The second side takes about half as long to cook. Serve steaming hot with margarine and sugar, with syrup, or with what you will.

SOURDOUGH WAFFLES. Mix a little thicker sponge than for flapjacks. Let stand overnight as usual. Save out the original amount of starter. To the remaining sourdough add:

> 1 teaspoon salt
> 2 tablespoons sugar
> ¼ cup liquid shortening
> 2 eggs
> 1 teaspoon baking soda

Stir the salt, sugar, and melted margarine or other shortening smoothly into the batter. If you have whole eggs, add the yolks; then fold in the beaten whites and the soda. If you are using dehydrated eggs, add them and the soda to the batter. Cook on a hot, greased waffle iron until brown.

SOURDOUGH MUFFINS. Set the sponge the evening before as for flapjacks. The next morning take out the original starter and handle as usual. To the remaining sourdough add:

> 1½ cups whole wheat flour
> ½ cup sugar
> 1 teaspoon salt
> ¼ cup skim milk powder
> 1½ teaspoons baking soda
> 1 cup raisins
> ½ cup liquid shortening
> 2 eggs

Mix flour, sugar, salt, powdered milk, and soda. Add either the raisins or perhaps blueberries or some similar wild fruit.

Make a cavity in the center of these blended ingredients. Mix the egg and the liquid shortening in this depression. Then stir only just enough to moisten everything.

Pour into greased muffin tins and bake in a hot oven or reflector baker for 20 minutes or until done. If the muffins become ready before the rest of the meal, loosen and tilt them in the pan, so that air can circulate around them, and lean them near the heat where they'll stay warm.

SOURDOUGH FRENCH BREAD. The nutty, toasty crustiness of this bread really goes well with the substantial fare on which hearty outdoor appetites thrive. To make 2 loaves you'll need:

> 1 cup water
> ½ cup milk
> 4 cups flour
> 2 teaspoons salt
> 2 tablespoons sugar
> 1½ tablespoons shortening
> 1½ cups sourdough starter

Bring water to a boil and mix with milk. Cool to lukewarm. Mix the flour with the salt and sugar in a large container. Make a bowl-like depression in the center.

Mix the lukewarm liquid with the sourdough starter in this well. Blend with the dry ingredients until you get a soft dough, but do not knead.

Cover and move to a warm place to rise until about double in bulk. This should take some 2 hours. Then turn out on a lightly floured mixing surface. This may be an easily carried sheet of plastic.

Roll half the dough into a large rectangle. Fold the 2 long sides toward the middle. Then roll together like a jelly roll. Do the same with the other half of the dough.

Sprinkle 2 tablespoons of corn meal lightly over the nearest thing you can come by in the way of a large greased baking sheet. Aluminum foil can be used. So can two large frypans. Place the loaves with their smoother sides uppermost. With a sharp knife make diagonal slits every couple of inches across the top of each loaf.

Now for the crust, take:

> 1 teaspoon cornstarch
> 1 teaspoon cold water
> ½ cup boiling water

Mix the cornstarch and cold water. Pour into the boiling water in a pan. Bring to a brief boil. Allow to cool. Then brush the loaves with it.

Now cover the loaves and place in a warm spot to double once more in bulk, which will usually take about another hour. Afterwards, brush the loaves a second time with the cornstarch mixture.

Commence baking in a hot oven or reflector baker for 15 minutes to set the crust. Then brush the loaves a third and final time with the cornstarch preparation. Reduce the heat to moderate and continue baking 30 minutes or until the bread is done and golden brown. Baking the bread longer, with less heat, will make for even thicker crust. The dutch oven really does a job with this bread.

CORN

CORN PONES. Mix two cups corn meal, 1 teaspoon salt, and 1 tablespoon shortening. Add enough milk, about 1 cup, to make a stiff dough. Shape into thin ovals. Bake in a hot oven or reflector baker a half hour or until rich brown.

ASH CAKES. Form the above dough into balls the size of eggs. Roll in flour, or wrap in foil or clean sweet leaves. Bury in hot ashes at the edge of the fire.

HUSH PUPPIES. Colonel Townsend Whelen makes these by mixing 2 cups yellow corn meal, ¾ cup flour, 2½ teaspoons baking powder, and 1 teaspoon salt with 1 cup water to make a medium thick dough. Drop big gobs into deep hot fat. Cook until a rich brown. Hush puppies are particularly good with fresh fish. In fact, the Colonel and a lot of us prefer cooking them in fat where fish and onions are also being fried.

GOLDEN CORN BREAD

    1 cup yellow corn meal
    1 cup flour
    ½ teaspoon salt
    2 teaspoons baking powder
    1 egg
    1 cup milk
    ¼ cup melted shortening or oil

Mix the corn meal, flour, salt, and baking powder as thoroughly as possible. Beat the egg and add the other liquids to it. Then combine everything, stirring just enough to moisten. Pour into a greased pan. Bake in a hot oven for half an hour.

FRYPAN CORN BREAD. Get this cooking a half hour before come-and-get-it time. For two hungry men you'll want:

    1 cup corn meal
    1 cup flour
    2 tablespoons sugar
    1 teaspoon salt
    2 teaspoons baking powder
    2 eggs
    4 tablespoons liquid shortening
    1 cup milk

Combine the dry ingredients. If using fresh eggs, beat them separately. Blend the eggs, shortening, and milk. Then quickly mix everything.

Pour the batter into a warm, well greased frypan. Cover and place immediately over low heat.

SPOON BREAD. This is the recipe that Colonel Whelen's daughter, Mrs. William G. Bowling, uses for spoon bread; good when eaten with butter or margarine along with the main dish instead of potato, and also when served with syrup to provide a special treat for dessert.

    2 cups milk
    ½ cup corn meal
    1 teaspoon salt
    1 tablespoon melted butter
    ½ teaspoon baking powder
    3 eggs

Scald the milk in a pan by heating it nearly to the boiling point. Stir in the corn meal bit by bit. Continue cooking for several minutes, stirring to avoid scorching. Then remove from the heat and add the salt, melted butter, baking powder, and the egg yolks beaten until light. Beat the egg whites stiff and fold them in.

Pour the batter into a buttered baking dish in which it will lie about 2 inches deep. Bake for 30 minutes or until the spoon bread is roofed with a thick brown crust.

CANOE BREAD. This went well on the most recent

deer hunting trip I took by canoe down the famous Half Moon of the Southwest Miramichi River, shortly before the New Brunswick freeze-up. Matter of fact, the hunting and the eating were so good that the ice caught us. I had to cache my canoe above Big Louie rapids and walk out to the railroad, and I've never had a chance to go back after it.

For enough hot bread for two of us, it took:

4 tablespoons shortening
1 teaspoon salt
¼ cup corn meal
2 teaspoons baking powder
1½ cups flour
½ cup water

The amount of flour was always approximate because we were spending as many hours as possible in the bush and shying away from any unnecessary culinary chores. We dropped the shortening in one gob in the top of the rolled-down flour sack. The salt, baking powder, and corn meal went atop it. Then the cook for that particular meal worked the ingredients into the lard, picking up whatever flour clung to them. He next dented the flour with his fist, poured in the ½ cup of water, and without any delay mixed a soft wad of dough.

Flattened, this went into a warm, greased frypan for cooking over birch coals. The salty, thick, brown crust always tasted particularly good after a hard, dehydrating day among the alders.

FLAPJACKS TO DUMPLINGS

FLAPJACKS FOR TWO. I ate these once with King Gething who, having forgotten his skillet, used a long-handled prospector's shovel instead. King first scoured the shovel in sand, then doused it in the Peace River, and finally swiped it lightly with a piece of bacon rind. The handle proved an unexpected convenience.

2 cups flour
2 teaspoons baking powder
½ teaspoon salt

>   2 tablespoons sugar
>   2 eggs
>   1½ cups milk
>   2 tablespoons liquid shortening

Combine the dry ingredients, including the powdered milk if that's what you have in camp. Beat the eggs if they are whole, and combine with the shortening and the fluid. Otherwise, reconstitute the dried eggs and combine in the same way. When everything is ready to go, mix the whole business very briefly into a thin batter. Overmixing will make these tough. For this reason, slightly lumpy batter is preferable to one that's beaten until smooth. Cook the same as sourdough flippers.

DUMPLINGS. Nothing sets off a hearty outdoor stew like steaming hot dumplings. These are a cinch to make, and they have the additional advantages of meaning neither separate cooking nor extra washing. The following recipe should satisfy two ravenous campers. About a dozen minutes before mealtime take:

>   2 cups flour
>   2 teaspoons baking powder
>   1 teaspoon salt
>   2 tablespoons margarine
>   1 cup milk

Mix the dry ingredients. Work in the margarine or other solid shortening. Make a bowl-like hollow in the center. Have everything ready to roll, for these dumplings should be cooked only 8 to 10 minutes, and then the meal should be served immediately. Have the broth simmering above enough meat and other solids so that the dumplings will not sink below the surface.

Now pour the milk into the well in the middle of the dry ingredients. Mix quickly and gently with a folding, rather than a stirring or whipping, motion.

Moisten a large spoon in the broth. Use it to place large spoonfuls, apart from one another, atop the stew. Cover tightly. After several minutes, you may if you want turn each dumpling carefully and speedily. Re-cover immediately and continue simmering until light and fluffy.

Then serve without delay. If any dumplings remain for second helpings, place them in a separate hot dish so they won't become soggy.

CORN MEAL DUMPLINGS. These are good for a change. To make the same amount as above, you'll need:

1½ cups corn meal
½ cup flour
2 teaspoons baking powder
1 teaspoon salt
3 eggs
¾ cup milk
2 tablespoons liquid shortening

Mix the dry ingredients. Beat the eggs, milk, and shortening together. Have the stew simmering and 15 minutes from being done. Or whenever you prefer with dumplings, which are actually drop biscuits cooked in boiling liquid, have broth seething in a wide stewpan.

Quickly blend the dumpling batter. As before, add it by the large, separate spoonful to the bubbling liquid. Cover tightly. Allow to simmer 15 minutes. Then remove the dumplings before they lose their featheriness.

CHAPTER 8

MAIN AND SIDE DISHES

BACON. "Bacon," a sourdough friend translated when asked what he meant by saying he'd gorged himself with vast quantities of *tiger*. "That's because it's striped. Sounds nobler when called tiger."

The main troubles that camp cooks experience with bacon arise from their submitting it too soon to too much heat. Not only is the bacon thus burned and toughened, but very often the frypan becomes a mass of leaping flames. Aside from resulting offenses to taste and digestion, this is wasteful if nothing worse. The nearly 3,000 calories per pound that fat side bacon contains lie largely in its grease, any excess of which should be saved, particularly in the bush.

We'll do better to start the bacon in a *cold* frypan and to fry it slowly over a very few coals raked to one side of the blaze. Move and turn the bacon from time to time. If you like it crisp, keep pouring off the grease. Don't waste any of this, though. It has numerous camp uses.

More satisfactory still is the practice of laying the strips well apart in a pan and baking them evenly to a golden brown in a moderately warm reflector baker.

Slabs of bacon have a tendency to mold. This mold can be harmlessly wiped off with a clean cloth moistened either in vinegar or in a solution of baking soda and water.

"BOILED" EGGS. Get enough water boiling in a pan to cover the eggs by an inch. Place the eggs in the pan with a spoon and let the temperature immediately drop to a simmer, keeping it that way until the eggs are done. With all egg dishes, moderate heat is necessary if you want to avoid toughness. Usual preferences here range between 2½ and 3½ minutes of cooking, depending on how stiff you like the whites. Remove and break open at once. Serve immediately, preferably in heated dishes.

HARD BOILED EGGS. Get things started the same way as above. Keep the eggs simmering, completely covered, for 8 to 10 minutes. Then remove from the heat and plunge into cold water. If the shells are cracked slightly before the eggs cool, peeling will be easier.

Campers sometimes get their hard boiled and raw eggs mixed. There's an easy way to tell the difference. If the egg will spin freely, it's cooked. The only condition that will cross you up is when the eggs are frozen.

POACHED EGGS. There's a gimmick to this one. Fill a frypan 2 inches deep with water, with roughly a teaspoon of salt for every 4 cups of water. Bring the water to the bubbling point. Then take a spoon and start the water revolving in one direction.

Now slide each egg gently into the water from a saucer. The movement of the liquid will keep the whites from spreading. Dip some of the water over the top. Three minutes of simmering suits most people. Or once the eggs are in, you may set the water off the heat for 5 minutes. Try these eggs sometime on a small mound of buttered rice, noodles, spaghetti, macaroni, or potatoes.

SCRAMBLED EGGS. The addition of milk has a tendency to toughen scrambled eggs. Instead, add 1 tablespoon of cold water for each egg. Mix the eggs and water well with salt and pepper to taste. Heat a tablespoon of fat in a frypan just hot enough to sizzle a drop of water. Pour in the egg mixture and reduce the heat. When the eggs have started to harden, begin stirring them constantly with a fork. Remove while they're still soft and creamy.

FRIED EGGS. Have about ½ inch of fat warm, not hot. Break in your eggs. Keeping the heat low so that the whites won't become tough and leathery, baste the yolks until they are well filmed. Salt, pepper, and serve on a hot plate.

Or get a tablespoon of fat just hot enough to sizzle a test drop of water. Break in the eggs. Take the frypan off the heat at once. Baste the eggs with hot fat 3 or 4 minutes.

OMELET. Break the eggs into a bowl or mixing dish. Add 1 teaspoon water for each egg. For a 3-egg omelet, season with ¼ teaspoon salt and just a dash of pepper.

Beat vigorously with a fork until yolks and whites are blended.

Melt 1 tablespoon butter (1 teaspoon for each egg) in a frypan until it just begins to brown. Pour in the eggs. Keep shaking and slanting the pan slightly while cooking so as to keep the omelet from sticking. As soon as the bottom of the omelet starts to harden, slip a thin spatula or knife well under the edges and lift the middle of the omelet so that uncooked egg can flow beneath it. This liquid egg, incidentally, will repair any resulting breaks and tears.

An omelet takes only about 5 minutes from shells to heated plates. It is done as soon as the eggs no longer run freely but the top still looks moist and creamy. Omelets will toughen if they are allowed to brown at all. Fold the omelet by tilting the pan sideways with one hand and then lifting the uppermost section about ⅓ over the middle. Now tilt, shake, and slide the folded omelet onto the hot plate. It's actually easier to make one such easily handled 3-egg omelet for each camper than to try to manipulate any more than, at most, a 6-egg omelet.

FRENCH TOAST. For half a dozen slices of hard bread, beat 3 eggs well. Add 1 cup of milk, 3 tablespoons sugar, and 1 teaspoon vanilla. Melt 3 tablespoons of margarine or other fat in a frypan. Dip each slice of bread in the egg mixture and brown lightly on both sides in the skillet. Sprinkle with cinnamon while hot and serve at once with sugar and margarine, tart jelly, or syrup.

TOMATOES, ONIONS, & EGGS. This nourishing and easily digestible dish, with the mild and provocatively elusive flavor, is unusually good when someone hauls into camp late, especially as its preparation is both simple and swift. Proportions, which are flexible, may be varied in ratio to appetite.

For two late arrivals, brown a couple of diced onions with a little grease in a frypan. When these have cooked to a dark blandness, add a small can of tomatoes. Let these begin to bubble. Then break in 6 eggs. Season with salt and pepper. Keep scrambling over low heat until fairly dry.

EGGS ON HORSEBACK. Rub your 2-pound, inch-thick

steak with salt, pepper, and a suggestion of mustard. Pan broil in a heavy frypan, searing quickly on both sides and then cooking more slowly until done to taste.

Meanwhile, melt 2 tablespoons of margarine or butter in another pan. Add 2 tablespoons chopped onion, a small can of mushroom sauce or ½ can of condensed mushroom soup if either is available, and 3 tablespoons of undiluted evaporated milk. When these are hot, fork in 6 eggs and, stirring, cook to the desired consistency. Or use powdered eggs and milk.

Trot the sizzling steak, cut in two, onto prewarmed plates. Saddle each half with the scrambled eggs. This recipe makes just enough breakfast for Colonel Whelen and me if no one else wanders into camp.

EGG IN A HOLE. Make a hole in the middle of a slice of bread or bannock. Toast one side of the slice with margarine or butter in a frypan. Turn over. Add more grease if the frypan seems dry. Then drop an egg into the hole and fry to suit, on one side only.

WHELEN SANDWICH. You'll need bacon, onion, eggs, cheese, seasoning, and patience enough to make seconds and maybe thirds. For each sandwich start 2 slices of bread toasting over the heat. Cut a slice of bacon into small bits. Fry these until they are crisp, pouring the excess grease into the camp shortening can. Fork the bacon together into a small rectangle and place a slice of onion atop it. Cook the onion until it begins to soften and tan.

Then break an egg over it. Puncture the yolk with the fork. Salt and pepper. Cover with a square of cheese. Cook slowly until the egg is done and the cheese has melted. Place each such serving between two slices of toast. If any watercress is handy, add several sprigs of that. With the average camp frypan you can usually have four such sandwiches going at once.

WELSH RABBIT. Melt 1 tablespoon margarine or butter in a pan. Add 1 tablespoon flour, ⅛ teaspoon pepper, and ¼ teaspoon salt. Mix thoroughly. Gradually stir in 2 cups of grated, shredded, or diced cheddar cheese, as aged and tangy as is available. Keep stirring over low heat until the cheese has melted. Heat ½ cup of milk and stir that in gradually and thoroughly. Add a slightly beaten fresh or reconstituted egg. Cook an additional 2 minutes. Serve at once on toast or hot crisp crackers.

APPLE CASSEROLE. Apples and cheese have always gone together, and this holds true when you combine them in a casserole. Special reflector baker and oven dishes such as the following help break the occasional monotony of cold rainy weather when your fire will be going anyway. You'll need:

          1 cup dried apples
         1½ cups water
         1½ cups soft bread crumbs
         1½ cups milk
          4 eggs
         1½ cups grated yellow cheese
          1 teaspoon salt
          ⅛ teaspoon black pepper
          ¼ teaspoon dried mustard
             paprika and dried parsley

Chop apples. Bring slowly to a boil in the water and simmer 5 minutes.

If the bread or bannock crumbs are not soft, soak them a few minutes in the milk. Beat the eggs well. Best cheese to use if you can is the old-fashioned yellow cracker-barrel variety, as sharp as you like. Mix the crumbs, milk, cheese, salt, pepper, and mustard. Add to the apples. Stir into the beaten eggs.

Pour into a shallow, well-greased baking dish. Bake in a moderately slow oven or reflector baker until the ingredients have become set and lightly browned on top. This should take about ½ hour. Sprinkle with paprika and dried parsley and call for everyone to heave to.

POOCH IN A POUCH. Let everyone impale a frankfurter, canned or fresh, on the peeled end of a sharpened green stick. Make some bannock dough (see chapter on breads). Roll out and cut into narrow, 5-inch-long ribbons. Or so mold a ball of dough between the palms. Spiral one of these strips around each of the "dogs." Press the dough firmly together at each end to hold it in place. Bake over the edge of a small campfire, turning slowly, for about 5 minutes or until done.

BAKED TOMATOES. Drain the juice from a large can of tomatoes. Use for beverage. Mix with the remaining solid portions: 1 cup cubed toast, 1 teaspoon salt, ½ cup sugar, and 2 tablespoons margarine. Spread this out in a greased pan or baking dish. Sprinkle with bread crumbs. Bake in a moderate oven or reflector baker 25 minutes.

NOODLES TO MACARONI

QUICK EGG NOODLES. Beat 2 eggs with ⅛ teaspoon salt until foamy. Blend with 4 tablespoons flour. Pour steadily in a thin stream into simmering broth, stirring all the time. Cook 2 minutes. Then serve immediately.

MACARONI, SPAGHETTI, NOODLES. A ¼ pound of any of these uncooked doubles in volume to about 2 cupfuls cooked and makes an average portion. Cook each such portion in 2 quarts of boiling water seasoned with 2 teaspoons salt.

Break the macaroni into small bits before cooking. Let the spaghetti and noodles gradually soften in contact with the boiling water and so adapt themselves to the pan. Stir occasionally to avoid sticking. Boil, uncovered, only until the macaroni or other paste is tender but still firm. Test by chewing. The time varies with different pastes but averages between 8 and 12 minutes. Drain immediately, as by holding the lid over the pan in such a way that just enough of an opening is left to allow the water to run off.

BAKED MACARONI AND CHEESE. Boil ½ pound macaroni in 4 quarts of water with 4 teaspoons of salt, according to the preceding directions. Cut ½ pound of cheese into cubes. Open a small can of tomatoes.

Alternate layers of cooked macaroni with cheese in a greased pan or baking dish, seasoning each layer with salt and pepper. Add 1 tablespoon of solid tomato to each layer. Then pour enough tomato over everything to come within ½ inch of the top. Roof with sliced onion if you want. Bake in a hot oven or reflector baker until well browned.

BEANS, ET AL

BEANS. The various dry beans and their cousins, the dry peas and lentils, are favorite old-time dehydrated foods. All provide hearty nourishment because of their carbohydrates which the body transforms into energy. They contain some B vitamins. Besides such minerals as iron and calcium, they furnish protein which the body needs for building and repairing its organs and tissues. They are, furthermore, both inexpensive and fairly easy to prepare.

Although split peas and lentils can be cooked without soaking, the ordinary beans may be soaked overnight. Preferably, however, they can be started by first bringing the water to a boil for 2 minutes. After they have then been soaked an hour, they will be ready to cook. The brief pre-cooking, too, will guard against any souring if they are to be soaked in warm weather. Cooking should then be done in the same water, so as to preserve flavor and to conserve vitamins and minerals.

Here is the whole story:

Start with 1 cup of	Soak in water	Add 1 teaspoon salt; boil gently	Will yield at least
Black beans	3 cups	About 2 hours	2 cups
Blackeye beans	2½ cups	½ hour	2½ cups
Cranberry beans	3 cups	About 2 hours	2 cups
Great Northern beans	2½ cups	1 to 1½ hours	2½ cups
Kidney beans	3 cups	About 2 hours	2¾ cups
Lentils	2½ cups (No soaking needed)	½ hour	2½ cups
Lima beans, large	2½ cups	1 hour	2½ cups
Lima beans, small	2½ cups	About 45 minutes	2 cups
Navy (pea) beans	3 cups	About 2½ hours	2½ cups
Peas, split	Best made into soup as they break up easily during cooking		
Peas, whole	2½ cups	1 hour	2½ cups
Pinto beans	3 cups	About 2 hours	2½ cups

CAMP BAKED BEANS. "Take 3 cups of dried navy beans. Pick out any small pebbles you may find. Soak the beans overnight in cold water, and the next morning put to boil in a large kettle with a tablespoon of salt. Boil for about

2½ hours, adding boiling water as the fluid level goes down.

"Then drop in about a dozen 1-inch cubes of salt pork or bacon with the rind on it. Keep bubbling for about an hour and a half more or until the individual beans are soft, but not mushy. You have been keeping about 2 inches of water on top of the beans in the kettle. This water is now the finest of bean soup. Pour most of it into another container and serve while hot, but leave enough so that the beans are still quite damp.

"Then, usually the next day, place these beans about 2 inches deep in a pan, shift the cubes of pork or bacon to the top, sprinkle a little sugar over the entire surface, and bake in a reflector baker or oven for an hour or more, until they become a little brown on top." (Colonel Townsend Whelen)

BAKED BEANS. Soak a pound of small dry beans along with 6 thinly sliced onions overnight in enough cold water to cover. The next morning cook below the boiling point until the beans are done. Add water if necessary.

Cut ½ pound bacon or salt pork into 1-inch cubes. Mix 1 cup sugar, 2 tablespoons dry mustard, and 1 cup catsup. Now place alternate layers of this, the beans and onions, and the meat in a pot. Save enough bacon or pork with which to top everything generously. Bake in a moderate oven or reflector baker until crusty brown.

QUICK-COOKING BEANS. But if you are bean hungry and don't want to waste that much time in camp, you can heat up a meal of processed and cleaned quick-cooking beans in a few minutes. Directions are given on the packages.

Like the old German Erbswurst, pea and bean powders now available also make excellent and filling soups with a minimum of time and trouble. Stir such concentrates into hot water and bring everything to a simmer, making the soup as thick or thin as you like.

HOPPING JOHN. Start this, suggests my friend, H. S. Mathews, by bringing ½ cup washed blackeye beans to a boil for 2 minutes in 3 cups water. Then cover and allow to soak 1 hour. Add ¼ pound diced bacon or salt pork. Simmer, covered, 1 hour or until the beans are tender. Add

½ cup raw rice, plus a dried hot red pepper if you have one, and cook another 15 minutes or until the rice is tender. Add boiling water if more liquid is needed. Season to taste. This is really something when a campfire leaps at dry spruce logs, and the stars come out one by one.

PEA SOUP. Now and then there are few things more delicious when the bunch gets home, cold and agreeably tired from a long day's hunt, than a bowl of thick, hot pea soup. This sort of thaws everyone out and loosens the stomach kinks in preparation for more thorough enjoyment of that roast or steak.

Fast cooking split peas, both green and yellow, are now available that save the bother of overnight soaking and over-tedious cooking. Let a pound of these simmer until tender in 4 cups of meat stock, or in bouillon made by dissolving 4 chicken bouillon cubes in 4 cups of water. Then crush the peas with a spoon or fork and continue simmering, covered, along with salt and pepper to taste and a finely chopped onion.

The finishing touch, as far as I'm concerned, is furnished by those small chunks of bacon or salt pork scattered through the savory hotness. Put these in now. Here's the place, too, for that flavor-filled bacon rind you've been wondering what to do with. When everything is cooked, keep the soup hot and ready on the back of the fire.

LENTILS. Barely cover 1 cup of quickly cooking lentils with cold water, season with ½ teaspoon salt, and simmer until just tender.

Start 4 shredded or chopped strips of bacon in a cold frypan. When there is enough fat, add 4 diced onions. Stirring, cook until soft. Then add the lentils and mix thoroughly. Cook slowly for 20 minutes, covered unless there is an abundance of liquid. Season with paprika, parsley flakes, and if necessary with a little additional salt.

CORN MEAL

CORN MEAL MUSH. Mix 1 cup of corn meal with 1 cup of cold water. Get 3 cups of water, seasoned with 1 teaspoon salt, bubbling diligently. Pour in the corn meal mixture slowly and stir for 5 minutes or until the combination has thickened. Move to low heat for 30 minutes and occasionally stir. If it becomes necessary to thin this, use boiling water. A double boiler is a handy gadget when you're making corn meal mush or polenta. It's often easy to contrive one, as by arranging several pieces of silverware in the bottom of a pan of boiling water and setting the mush pot atop those.

If you prefer a thicker mush to begin with, use a total of 2 cups of water for every 1 cup of meal. Such mush may also be used with margarine as a vegetable, sliced cold for frying, or topped with molasses and milk for dessert.

POLENTA. Mix 1 cup yellow corn meal with 1 cup cold water and 1 teaspoon salt. Now get 3 cups of water simmering. Gradually stir in the corn meal mixture. Then, moving to the low heat, stir constantly about 5 minutes or until thickened.

Now pour a small layer into the bottom of a greased pan. Cover with liberal spoonfuls of canned tomatoes. Pour in more corn meal mush and top this time with slices of cheese. Do this until you have at least 4 layers. Finish off if you want with some sliced onions. Place in an oven or reflector baker and bake for 45 minutes or until the cheese has melted.

SCRAPPLE. "Take the head of a pig, wild boar, peccary, or any of the deer tribe. Remove eyes and tongue, then boil head in enough water to barely cover until the meat comes off the bones. Remove the meat from the stock, and let both cool, skimming most of the grease off the stock; strain the stock. Take 2 pounds of corn meal for every 3 pounds of meat. Bring the stock to a boil, slowly stir in the corn meal and cook to a medium-thick mush, adding a little hot water to thin it if there is not enough stock. Mix into each pound of meat ½ teaspoon salt, ¼ teaspoon black pepper, and a teaspoon of onion juice. Add the seasoned meat to the mush and cook in a double boiler for an hour. Then pour it into a greased pan and let it cool. To serve, cut this scrapple loaf into slices about ⅓ inch thick, like slices of bread, and fry until brown in a little bacon fat. Serve very hot. I had scrapple for breakfast twice a week for the first 21 years of my life. Fine grub." (Colonel Townsend Whelen)

RICE

The quickly cooking rices are a particular boon to outdoor cooks. Just follow the brief directions on the package.

Or if you want to boil some of the old fashioned variety, rub ½ cup of rice between the fingers in several changes of cold water, or in cold running water, until the water stays clear. Drain. Get 4 cups of water boiling briskly, put in 1 tablespoon salt, and then gradually add the rice. Lift the rice now and then with a spoon or fork to discourage sticking. Boil 20 minutes or until tender. Easy way to test is by biting or by rubbing a kernel between the fingers. There should be no hard spot in the center. Drain, saving the water for soup or mulligan. Rinse with hot water. Place the resulting 1½ cups or so of boiled rice near the fringes of the fire to dry.

CAMP RICE. Just what old trail cook Ted Boynton accomplished with rice would have been enough to assure his popularity with any pack horse outfit. Hewn down to indoor proportions for my wife's benefit, Ted's favorite recipe in that category went:

"Hack up 2 large onions and a fist-sized chunk of sow belly. That's salt pork, Vena, though bacon will do. Brown 'em a mite in a kettle. Add 2 cups of b'iling water and a cup of rice. B'il rice until soft. Don't do no stirring, for cripe's sake.

"Excuse me . . . Well, er, be heating half a big can of tomatoes, a teaspoon of salt, a tablespoon of sugar maybe, a teaspoon of celery seed if any's in camp, and a pinch of black pepper which with my hands is a quarter-teaspoon. Add these to the cooked rice. Sprinkle on grated cheese like . . . like aitch. Then you sure don't want no lost dudes wandering into camp for awhile."

OVEN RICE. Measure 2 cups boiling water into a pan

or baking dish. Add ½ teaspoon salt. Stir in 1 cup rice. Cover and bake in a moderate oven or reflector baker about 35 minutes or until tender.

FRIED RICE. The nutty flavor of this is so good with such repasts as steaks, chops, and fried grouse that sometimes you don't know in which direction to reach first for seconds. Stir and cook 2 cups boiled rice in 2 tablespoons fat in a frypan over low heat for about 5 minutes. Add 2 tablespoons chopped, preferably green onions and if you want a similar volume of cooked meat chopped and shredded into tiny bits. Cook this several minutes longer. Then break in 1 egg. Season with 2 teaspoons soy sauce or with salt to taste. Stir vigorously until the egg is set.

RICE WITH GAME. For rice with rabbit and other small game, melt 2 tablespoons margarine or butter in a pan. Add a chopped small onion, stirring until tender and tan. Gradually add 1 cup rice, shaking until the grains are coated with fat. Cook until lightly browned. Add 2 cups of the hot stock, cover, and simmer until the liquid is absorbed and the rice tender. Spread on the individual plates, add a slab of butter to each portion, and top with the meat.

GREEN RICE. Melt 2 tablespoons margarine or butter in a pan. Stir a chopped small onion in this until it is lightly browned. Add 2 cups cooked rice, 1 cup warm milk, and 1 tablespoon powdered parsley.

Beat 2 eggs with a fork. Mix with 1 teaspoon salt and 1 cup grated, shredded, or cubed cheese. Add these to the above. Mix thoroughly. Bake in a moderate oven or reflector baker for about 45 minutes or until firm.

Or try this version. Mix 2 cups of hot cooked rice with 2 tablespoons melted margarine and 1 tablespoon powdered parsley. If you can come by them, add small amounts of shredded watercress, young mustard, or dandelion leaves, etc. Season the savory result with salt to taste and serve.

PILAFF. Stir 1 cup raw rice in 3 tablespoons shortening in a frypan over low heat until the rice begins to tan. A small, chopped onion may also be included. Season with salt and pepper. Then pour on 2 cups broth or bouillon. Canned soup may be used instead, mushroom being a tasty choice. Cover the frypan and simmer over very low heat for about 30 minutes until the rice is tender and almost dry. If the rice is nearly dry, however, and is still hard in the center, add a bit more hot liquid and cook as long as necessary. Top with butter or margarine.

RISOTTO. Saute 2 small chopped onions in 3 tablespoons of shortening until soft. Add 1½ cups of the more solid parts of a can of tomatoes and stir and heat until bubbling. Add 3 cups of broth or bouillon, 1 teaspoon salt, and 1 cup raw rice. Cook covered over low heat for about 30 minutes or until the rice is tender and almost dry. Stir in ½ cup of shredded or grated cheese, sprinkle with paprika and powdered parsley, and serve hot.

WILD RICE. Wash this well in cold water. Stir ½ cup into 2 cups of boiling water, seasoned with ½ teaspoon salt. Cover and simmer without stirring for about 30 minutes or until the wild rice is tender.

Only drawback to this delicacy, unless you harvest it yourself for free, is the expense of the purple-black seed with its smoky sweetness, so excellent with game and poultry. However, there are a couple of other ways to approach the same distinctive flavor you'd come by after a hard day of harvesting this seed of tall freshwater grasses.

For one: mix 2 cups of regular hot boiled rice with ½ cup of hard bread or bannock crumbs that have been browned in 3 tablespoons of margarine or butter. Salt and pepper to taste.

For the other: if you happen to be in New Mexico or other pinon country when pine nuts are ready, gather a quantity of these. Then mix 1 cup of regular boiled brown rice with 1 tablespoon melted butter or margarine, salt and pepper to taste, and 2 tablespoons shelled pine nuts. I ate this first in the shadows of the tall Sangre de Cristo Mountains where a century before Kit Carson had likely sat down to some of the same.

A FASCINATING INTEREST

When the family is away on vacation together is an appropriate time for the cooks of the household to take as much of a rest as possible from culinary cares. One way to do this, while maintaining satisfactory relations with both appetites and digestions, is by scheduling a series of simple though hearty dishes.

Here are a few that not only fulfill these specifications but which have the added enhancement of combining tradition and color. They are special recipes of the North, so termed by the Hudson's Bay Company which, incorporated May 2, 1670, was already a century old before the United States was more than an absent-minded dent in one of Paul Revere's teapots.

"There is no mystery about cooking," this world's oldest trading corporation assures the future managers of its present fur trading posts, in cooking classes where the following dishes are among those shown to be quickly and easily prepared with materials normally available in out-of-the-way places. "You can become a good cook with a little practice, a dash of patience, and a pinch of common sense. Cooking can be a fascinating interest!"

ONE DISH MEAL. Variations on this theme are numerous, but here's a favorite at many H.B.C. trading posts.

1   can kidney or lima beans
1   can tomatoes
1   can sausages
1   small onion, chopped

Grease a baking pan. Combine the above in it. Season with salt, pepper, and 1 teaspoon sugar. Sprinkle with bread or bannock crumbs. Bake in a moderate oven 20 to 30 minutes.

CHEESE BALLS. Grate or chop preferably dry, stale cheese. Mix it with an equal volume of flour. Add salt and pepper to taste, ½ teaspoon mustard, and bind with a well beaten egg. Drop by the spoonful into hot fat and fry until a light brown. In the Far North they serve these over boiled macaroni, topped with tomato sauce hot from the fire.

STOVIES. Put 1 tablespoon of bacon drippings, margarine, or such in a frypan or baking dish. Peel 5 potatoes and slice them into the utensil. Salt and pepper to taste, cover tightly, and cook atop the heat or in an oven or reflector baker until tender, stirring occasionally. When the potatoes are nearly done, slice or dice one of the canned meats, add this to the potatoes, and finish cooking.

VEGETABLE CASSEROLE. You can get this started in a hurry by opening small cans of peas, corn, and tomatoes. You'll also need a cup of bread, bannock, or cracker crumbs, seasoned with 1 teaspoon salt and ⅛ teaspoon pepper. Arrange the vegetables in layers. Sprinkle each layer with the seasoned crumbs. Dot the top with margarine or crisscross it with strips of bacon. For a one-dish meal, cut any of the canned meats into small pieces and include layers of this. Bake 25 minutes in a moderate oven or reflector baker.

BADGER SQUAWS. Cut the contents of a small jar of dried beef into small pieces. Add to it ¼ cup of milk and 1 can of corn. Heat thoroughly. This goes well with crisp, fresh crackers.

IRISH SCALLOP. This is the Arctic Circle version. You'll need: 2 boiled potatoes, salt and pepper, and a can apiece of corned beef, mixed carrots and peas, and tomato soup. Grease a pan or baking dish. Spread the corned beef over the bottom. Cover with the carrots and peas, adding a little of the liquor and saving the rest for some other use. Slice the boiled potatoes over this. Salt and pepper to taste. Pour the can of tomato soup over everything. Bake in a moderate oven or reflector baker ½ hour.

TRAVELING WINTER TRAILS

On an outdoor trip anywhere, especially across ice and snow in weather so cold that the breath makes a continual fog, food is a consideration second only to water. The more drastic the conditions that may be encountered, the more essential it will be to plan the meals intelligently beforehand.

On short enough journeys, time and effort on the trail can be saved by cooking as much of the food as possible before heading into the whitened wilderness. You may find it worthwhile, too, to keep ahead of your appetite all the way by cooking the next day's meals at the previous night's camp. This is particularly true in regions where fuel is scarce, as high above the timber line or in the northern Land of Little Sticks.

Certain dried foods, augmented so as better to meet winter conditions, may as well be carried ready mixed. Flour, baking powder, margarine, salt, and sugar can be stowed in closed containers in proportions for individual bannocks. (See chapter on breads.) In extremely cold weather, use more than the accustomed amount of shortening in these bannocks to provide extra nourishment and to prevent the breadstuff from freezing hard. You'll appreciate a larger proportion of sugar, too.

Here are a few suggestions for rations for winter trails, tried personally above the frost-furred tree line in tall country or up under the aurora borealis in the Far North. They are recommended, too, by the Hudson's Bay Company for use by its own men in and about the red-roofed trading posts it still operates in the North.

ONE-DISH BEAN STEW. Bean stew makes a nourishing and palatable dish, particularly when the still white cold is so extreme that wood smoke, instead of coiling out of sight, spreads above the campfire like an enormous banner. The preparation of this one-dish meal is commenced back at the base by soaking dried beans overnight. Partially bake or boil these. Mix in any kind of fresh or canned meat cut into very small segments. Add canned tomatoes. Flavor with molasses, spices, and if you want with beef extract.

Cook until the beans and meat are well done. Then pour the mixture into a shallow pan and allow to freeze. When frozen, break into small pieces and carry in a cotton bag. To use, simply heat what you want in a pan along with a little water.

When carrying frozen foods under such conditions, be sure to keep them frozen hard until they are required for use. Do not take any more of an item than you immediately require into a heated place. Leave the remainder in the cold, out of the way of hungry animals both small and large.

CARRYING FOOD IN COLD WEATHER. Any bacon should be sliced before one sets off on such a trip. It may also be partly cooked beforehand. The slices, in either event, can be frozen separately and carried this way until needed. Potatoes freeze into something resembling marble, so if you want to pack along some of these, boil them until they are a bit on the hard side. Slice thinly and put out to freeze in individual pieces. Carry the frozen chips in a cotton food sack. They will go well heated in the fat from fried bacon.

MEAT BALLS. Meat balls will provide another one-dish repast. Mince up venison or any kind of meat. Add a little milk, some bread crumbs, potatoes or any other vegetables you want, and whatever spices you prefer. Grated cheese and tomato catsup add to the taste. Shape into flattened meat balls. Partially cook and then freeze them. They will be ready to eat on short notice on the trail or in camp. Merely thaw them out and heat them in a pan with some water. You can prepare fish balls in the same general manner, substituting fresh or canned fish for the meat.

CEREAL

Prepare according to the instructions on the package.

A favorite camp cereal of a lot of us is oatmeal. The quickly cooking variety saves time. Way I do is ready it the night before by adding ½ cup oatmeal and ½ teaspoon salt to 2 cups cold water. A ¼ cup of raisins, more or less, plump out overnight to add flavor. The next morning I hunch far enough out of the sleeping bag to get the fire going, put on the covered pan, and let the contents come to a boil before setting it to one side for a few minutes. Then I either pour in evaporated milk straight out of the can, or in colder weather add a liberal spoonful of margarine, and begin satisfying the inner man.

This is really luxury when deepening cold has condensed, close above the throbbing earth, a twinkling ceiling of ice crystals to which the smoke of your solitary campfire ascends in an unwavering pillar.

CHAPTER 9

THE VEGETABLE STORY

BAKED POTATOES. A good way to cook this native American vegetable is to bake the large ones in their skins in hot ashes, not glowing coals, until they become pretty well blackened on the outside. They're done when a thin, sharpened stick will run through their middles easily. Rake out, break in half, and serve at once with margarine and salt.

A more complicated way to go about this on occasion, in camps near civilization, is to cut well scrubbed potatoes lengthwise into 3 slabs. Lay thin slices of onion, salted and peppered, between these sections. Then reassemble each potato, wrap in a sheet of heavy foil or several thicknesses of lightweight foil, and bake in a nest of ashes among hot coals for about a half hour or until done, turning once during this period.

Potatoes may be scrubbed, rubbed with melted fat or salad oil, pricked with a fork, (or prepared as above and held together with skewers) and baked in a hot oven or reflector baker. This method is handiest when combined with some other cooking, as about an hour of baking is required.

BOILED POTATOES. Scrub enough potatoes, choosing those of equal size as far as possible so they'll cook uniformly. Cover with boiling water, seasoned with 1 teaspoon salt for every 3 potatoes. Simmer, covered, 20 to 30 minutes or until an inserted fork indicates they're tender. Drain, peel if you wish, season with salt and pepper, and cover to keep warm and to prevent sogginess.

Or, particularly if you're in a hurry, peel. Cut into uniform pieces. Drop into cold water for a short time to prevent darkening. Cook, covered, in a small amount of boiling salted water until done. Then handle as above.

MASHED POTATOES. If you're going to mash your

potatoes, peel and slice them rather thin. Boil in salted water until very well done. Drain and return to the heat until the remainder of the water has evaporated. Mash—a round bottle being a handy backwoods implement at this stage. Salt to taste. Sprinkle on a few flakes of pepper. Add 1 tablespoon melted margarine, and if you want ¼ cup hot milk for every 2 medium-size potatoes or their equivalent. Whip with a fork until fluffy. Top with a little paprika and powdered parsley, if you have any, and serve at once.

POTATO CAKES. An easy way to make potato cakes is to shape cold mashed potatoes as desired, then to cook them slowly in margarine or drippings, turning once, until they are tan and crusty.

POTATO ROULETTES. Add ¼ cup milk, 4 tablespoons grated or shredded cheese, and your idea of enough salt and pepper to 2 cups mashed potatoes. Beat until light. Drop by the spoonful into a greased pan. Bake in moderate oven or reflector baker.

FRIED POTATOES. "The most tasty way I know of to fry camp potatoes," opines my writing partner, Colonel Whelen, "is first to boil them peeled for 20 minutes, then to slice them into ¾ inch cubes. Have ¼ inch of lard or other cooking fat sizzling in the frypan. Put in several onions that have been chopped up fine. Before these have become much more than a light brown, add the cubed potatoes while the grease is still very hot.

"Now remove the frypan to a part of the fire where the fat will just simmer. Cover with a lid or tin plate. Let the contents bubble and cook in their own steam, occasionally giving them a turn with a spoon. Add salt and plenty of black pepper. Serve just before the potatoes begin to get hard on the outside."

FRYPAN POTATOES. Start 3 slices of bacon in a cold frypan and cook until crisp. Remove the bacon and pour all but a tablespoon of the drippings into the camp shortening can. Add a sliced and chopped onion, forking the bits around until they have started to brown. Break up the bacon and return it to the pan. Slice in 4 potatoes.

Flatten out the slices and cover them at once with a

minimum amount of water. Bring this to a simmer and keep
the potatoes cooking until they've started to break to pieces
and to thicken the liquid. Add hot water if any more is
required. Salt, pepper, and eat as soon as the potatoes are
ready.

HASHED BROWN POTATOES. Heat 4 tablespoons
margarine, cooking oil, or other shortening in the frypan.
Add enough potatoes, peeled and cut very fine. Salt and
pepper. Then press down and cook over low heat until
brown and crisp on the bottom. Loosen this crust with a
knife. Then cover the frypan with a plate and invert it
quickly, so that the potatoes will come out with the brown
underside on top.

POTATO BALLS. Cut into very small pieces 2 large,
peeled, raw potatoes and 1 small onion. Beat an egg with
½ teaspoon salt. Mix everything thoroughly and drop by
the tablespoonful into hot, deep fat. Remove when brown,
drain, and serve hot.

POTATO AND ONION PUFF. Cook equal quantities
of potato and onion together. Mash. Add milk, margarine,
and 1 or 2 well-beaten eggs. Beat until fluffy. Season with
salt and pepper. Spoon into a greased pan. Top with grated
or sliced cheese if you want. Bake until browned.

HASH. Colonel Whelen hustles together hash by chopping
cooked meat with an equal volume of boiled potatoes. Salt
and pepper to taste, and add one or all of the following:
chopped onion, fresh or powdered celery, and parsley flakes.
Moisten the mixture with soup stock, bouillon, thin milk, or
water. Spread thickly on a greased pan. Set over slow heat
20 minutes until the bottom of the hash is well browned, or
cook in a reflector baker with moderate heat.

BAKED HASH.

      1   can corned beef
      2   cups cold boiled rice
      3   diced raw potatoes
      1   can tomato soup
      ¼   cup bread crumbs
          salt and pepper
          margarine

Break up the corned beef with a fork. One of the other canned meats may be used instead, of course, in which case it may be easier to cube it. Place the meat, rice, and diced raw potatoes in alternate layers in a greased pan or baking dish. Season well. Empty a can of tomato soup over them. Sprinkle the top with ¼ cup of bread crumbs, dot with margarine, and bake in a moderate oven 20 minutes.

POTATOES H.B.C. Chop 5 or 6 cold boiled potatoes very fine and arrange them in a greased baking pan. You'll also need:

2	tablespoons margarine
1	tablespoon flour
1½	cups milk
¼	teaspoon pepper
1	teaspoon salt
1	egg
¼	cup grated cheese
¼	cup dry crumbs
1	tablespoon melted margarine

Make a cream sauce of the margarine, flour, milk, and seasonings. Add the egg and grated cheese. Pour this sauce over the potatoes, allowing it to run through the pieces. Cover with buttered crumbs, made by melting a tablespoon of margarine and mixing this gently with a fork into ¼ cup of dry bread, cracker, or bannock crumbs. Bake in a hot oven or reflector baker 15 minutes.

POTATO PANCAKES. Here is an old German way of making potato pancakes which are especially delicious outdoors, particularly when served with such wild fare as roast goose or venison pot roast. "They aren't the lightest food in the world," admits Duncan Hines who suggested them to me. "But like most German cookery they impart to the diner a feeling of solidity that is not quite heaviness. If I were to describe it in a word (and I am not by any means sure that I can) the word would be 'honest,' for it fills the hollow spaces and it is good and, after all, what more can we ask of food?"

1½	pounds raw potatoes, peeled
2½	tablespoons flour

1   teaspoon salt
2   eggs beaten
3   slices bacon, diced (optional)
   vegetable shortening

"Grate the potatoes and drain off the juice. Add the remaining ingredients to the potatoes and mix well. In a pan, heat enough shortening to make ¼ inch. The shortening should be sizzling hot. Drop the potato mixture from a spoon into the hot fat. Fry, turning once, until golden brown on both sides. Dry on absorbent paper and serve with applesauce."

POTATO SALAD. Here's my favorite year-around recipe for potato salad, unless you already have one of your own. For use as a main dish for 2 people, scrub and boil 6 medium potatoes, removing them from the salted water while they're still hard. Peel as sparingly as possible so as to preserve the utmost flavor and nourishment. Hard boil 6 eggs at the same time; then plunge them under cold water and peel them.

Slice some of the hot potato into an earthenware bowl, if one is at hand, or into whatever else is handy. Slice some egg atop it. Now pour on a liberal amount of preferably olive oil or of salad oil. Douse on about ¼ as much vinegar. Salt and pepper. Sprinkle on a very small amount of powdered garlic if you have any and if you don't object to it. Paprika and dried parsley will add eye and taste appeal. Repeat, keeping on doing this until you've used all the potatoes and eggs. Cover so that the flavor will permeate everything.

Preparing this salad half a day or more ahead of time will give the best results. Take off the lid once or twice and carefully, so as not to break up the eggs and potatoes, spoon the mixture around a bit to redistribute the oil and vinegar.

BOILED ONIONS. Peel the onions. These will cook more uniformly if all are about the same size. Large onions may be sliced before boiling. If you want, carry on these operations with the vegetables held under water.

Cover with salted boiling water. Cook, uncovered, some

20 to 35 minutes or until the onions are tender but not broken. The water, incidentally, will be excellent for soups and such. Drain, add your idea of enough butter or margarine, and season with salt and pepper.

ONION SOUP. A good time to make this is when you have plenty of broth on hand from game. Or you can use canned beef bouillon, bouillon cubes, etc.

Saute 2 large sliced onions very slowly in 2 tablespoons of margarine or butter. When they are just barely tender, but not brown, add 4 cups of broth or bouillon. Simmer slowly for 20 minutes. Season to taste with salt and pepper. Either serve as is or, if you've plenty of provisions and would like to start the meal off with something a little special, with the solids strained out to leave a clear soup.

ONION SOUP AU GRATIN. Saute 2 large, sliced onions very slowly in 2 tablespoons of margarine or butter. When they have become lightly browned, add 4 cups of broth, canned bouillon, or water in which 4 beef or chicken bouillon cubes have been dissolved. Salt to taste. Then simmer 15 minutes.

In the meantime, cut a substantial slice of preferably sourdough bread for everyone. Spread lightly with prepared mustard if you want. Cover with grated or sliced cheese and toast until crisp in the reflector baker or oven. If no reflector baker or oven is available, the bread can be toasted on anything from a campfire grate to a forked green stick, then turned, covered on the hot side with cheese, and very slowly toasted on the other side until crisp throughout. Put each slice in a bowl, breaking the toast into bits if necessary, and cover with the hot soup.

ONION SAUCE. An easy way to make this is to combine a package of dehydrated onion soup mix with 2½ cups of boiling water. Cover and simmer 10 minutes. In the meantime, stir 2 tablespoons flour into ½ cup cold water. Add this bit by bit to the simmering mix. Cook, stirring, until sufficiently thickened.

WHITE SAUCES. For the fat in these white sauces, a good idea is to use margarine, butter, and sometimes bacon drippings for extra flavor if the sauce is to be combined with mildly flavored foods. One of the bland cooking fats or oils will be entirely satisfactory if the sauce is to be used with more highly flavored foods.

	Thin	Medium	Thick
Milk:	1 cup	1 cup	1 cup
Flour:	1 tablespoon	2 tablespoons	3 to 4 tablespoons
Fat:	1 tablespoon	1 to 2 tablespoons	2 to 3 tablespoons

Melt the fat. Blend in the flour to make a smooth mixture. Slowly add the milk and cook over very low heat until thickened, stirring constantly. Add salt to taste, about ¼ teaspoon of salt per cup of milk usually being sufficient. Then cook 3 to 5 minutes longer, stirring occasionally.

ROAST CORN. You'll want sweet, young corn for this. Carefully strip the husks down to the end of the ear, leaving them attached. Pull off the silk. Soak the corn in cold salted water for ½ hour. Drain. Then brush the kernels with margarine or butter and sprinkle them with salt and a little pepper. Pull the husks back up around the corn and twist tightly together. Make a hollow of coals at the edge of the campfire, cover it with an inch of ashes, lay in the corn, cover with more ashes and then hot coals, and roast about ½ hour. Peel the husks back again and use as a handle.

If you're where there is green corn, probably aluminum foil is available, too. If you want, then, wrap and twist each ear tightly in foil before consigning it to the ash-insulated coals. This way you can poke the corn around occasionally to assure more even cooking, and even take a look, while it is roasting to taste.

VEGETABLES IN GENERAL

Few raw vegetables except for potatoes, onions, occasional corn and such, and the wild varieties detailed in a separate chapter are cooked in most vacation camps. The following general table, therefore, will save you time and trouble.

As you no doubt already know, heating fresh vegetables destroys a certain amount of their food value, so they should be cooked as quickly as possible and only until tender. Some of the valuable food elements also seep out into water, so vegetables should be boiled in the least possible amount of fluid, and this liquid should be used for soups, sauces, gravies, beverages, etc. Leafy vegetables, in fact, may profitably be lifted directly from the rinse into the pan and cooked without added water. Otherwise, start the vegetables in boiling water to reduce cooking time. The pan should ordinarily be covered.

If the vegetables are left in large pieces, fewer of the important nutrients will either oxidize or escape. Though washing is essential, vegetables should not be allowed to soak. A small brush is a help, for cooking in skins whenever possible will retain the maximum goodness. Potatoes, for example, are preferably scrubbed and boiled or baked with the skins intact. Matter of fact, a lot of us prefer eating skins and all except, of course, when the hide is badly charred from roasting in the campfire.

As for the practice of adding baking soda to vegetables, this is a prime destroyer of vitamins. The way many of us chronic wood loafers figure, if you're going to the trouble of fetching and preparing vegetables, you may as well get the maximum good out of them.

TIMETABLE FOR COOKING VEGETABLES

Vegetable	Boiling Minutes	Baking (Hot Oven) Minutes
Artichokes, French	20-30	
Jerusalem	15-25	
Asparagus (whole or butts)	10-25	
(tips)	5-15	
Beans, green wax (whole, pieces)	15-25	
Beans, lima	20-30	
Beets, young (small, whole)	30-45	40-60
mature (small, whole)	45-90	60-120
Beet greens	5-15	
Broccoli (stalks & buds)	8-25	
Brussels sprouts (whole)	8-20	
Cabbage, green (quarters)	5-15	
green (shredded)	3-10	
Cabbage, red (shredded)	8-12	
Carrots, young (whole)	10-25	35-45
young (sliced)	8-20	30-40
Carrots, mature (whole)	20-30	60
mature (sliced)	12-20	

Cauliflower (whole)	10-20	
(flowerets)	8-10	
Celery	10-20	
Chard, Swiss	10-25	
Corn, on cob	5-15	
Eggplant (sliced)	10-20	
Endive, curly	10-20	
Kale	10-25	
Kohlrabi (sliced, quarters)	20-40	
Leeks	12-35	
Okra (sliced)	10-30	
Onions, green (scallions)	8-15	
mature (quarters, whole)	20-35	50-60
Parsnips (quarters, whole)	10-30	30-45
Peas, green	5-20	
Potatoes, Irish (medium, whole)	20-40	45-60
Potatoes, Irish (quartered)	15-25	
Potatoes, sweet (whole)	20-35	30-45
sweet (quartered)	15-25	
Rutabagas (sliced, diced)	20-30	
Salsify (sliced, cubed)	15-20	
Spinach	5-10	
Squash, winter, Hubbard (pieces)	20-40	40-60
winter, Acorn (halves)	10-20	60
summer (sliced, halves)	10-20	30
Tomatoes	15-20	15-30
Turnips (whole, halves)	20-40	
(slices, cubes)	10-30	
Turnip greens	10-25	

CHAPTER 10

EATING FOR FREE

Think back to your really memorable camping, fishing, and hunting vacations. Isn't there a double-barreled combination that points up every one of them? It doesn't much matter if you were tenting in one of the national parks, stalking whitetails Down East, tracking grizzly in pelting Spring snows, or surf casting with the family for Pacific yellowtail. Wasn't a large part of the fun: (1) the grub, (2) and the kind of appetite that let you enjoy it!

Ever notice something else? Maybe you're one of the tribe who don't go much for liver most of the year. If so, how about breakfast the morning after you've been the first warrior in camp to bag a deer? Do you periodically listen to family complaints about fish bones during the workaday weeks? Then doesn't the conversation take a turn after the wife and kids have had a hand in filling that platter with bluegills?

Here's another thing you can mark down in your diary. The same deal will even work with spinach, when it's a wild spinach and you've gathered it yourself.

It will also work with numerous other wild vegetables and fruits. These grow everywhere. If you pack your rods and rifles far enough North, as a matter of fact, there is no nonedible vegetation whatsoever with the exception of one breed of mushrooms. Some of the lichens are bitter, it's true. But when this acidity is soaked out, such a variety as the familiar Iceland Moss is so nutritious that it's packaged and widely sold as food and tonic for convalescents.

The pick of the wild foods will upgrade your meals while you're fishing, hunting, or camping. That's not all. Back home they'll keep right on guaranteeing you some of the best eating there is—plus the continued incentive to get outdoors in the woods and fields, where the really healthy appetites are born.

172

PICK INSTEAD OF PACK. A lot of times you want to get a few miles deeper into remote country where the hunting and fishing are better. The outfit you're packing is just too heavy, however. So, reluctantly, you settle for less. This usually means you have to work harder for even the small ones. As for those record-busting trophies, they're just not around.

The next time, you figure, you're going to travel lighter and farther. With careful planning you find you can save weight and space on nearly every item in your outfit. When it comes to grub, though, you're still going to need a minimum of 2¼ pounds of reasonably waterfree provisions each day to keep enjoying yourself under full power.

Yet there's a way you can reasonably lop a pound a day off those basic food requirements and still have the rugged, tasty, healthy meals you need to make it a real vacation. This is a method once used by our frontiersmen and still employed today by sportsmen, explorers, and other experienced outdoorsmen who regularly journey into the most inaccessible regions of this continent. It's a technique you can adopt with every assurance of success from the start. I know, for I've used it with increasing satisfaction for the past two decades.

The grubstake I generally pack on extended hunts when space and weight are at a premium includes: flour, oatmeal, side bacon, oleomargarine, sugar, salt, rice, jam, tea, and either baking powder for bannock or baking soda for sourdough. For those days when game is going to keep me pretty well occupied, I add a few of the dehydrated vegetables and fruits.

What about the sacks of onions and spuds, that bag of oranges, the bunches of celery, odd cabbages and cauliflowers, lemons, carrots, parsnips, and the occasional head of lettuce I used to try to keep in a moistened cloth bag just a couple days longer? They stay where they are until I get back to where transportation is no longer a problem. So do those heavy cans of berries. Why bother with the bulk, heft, care, waste, and expense of such vegetables and fruits when you can pick them as you need them?

Besides meaning the difference between an easy pack and a troublesome one, adding from season to season the recognition of a couple more wild edibles can become an engrossing and practical hobby, as well as a thrifty and healthful way of introducing new delicacies to the table. You don't even have to lug your pots and pans into wilderness country to begin finding wild eatables. They grow everywhere.

There are actually thousands of wild eatables, far too many to cover in this chapter. If you are particularly interested in the subject, however, you'll find quite a few pictured and discussed in my Stackpole book devoted entirely to the problems suggested by the title, *Living Off the Country*. A very large number, along with detailed drawings, also appear in another of my books published by the Stackpole Company, *How To Go Live in the Woods on $10 a Week*.

You don't need to be any sort of an expert to begin taking immediate advantage of this free grub. There are so many edible wild fruits and vegetables, in fact, that their very number scares off a lot of people before they start. There's no good reason for this last. Recognizing a half dozen or so will do the trick. That's all of a choice many old woodsmen bother with, anyway.

As far as that goes, just about every camper, fisherman, and hunter reading this already knows at least a dozen wild eatables, although perhaps not as sources of nourishment. You're afraid you may be an exception? Then here's a tip. Don't wager any folding money against yourself until we've had a look at some of the more widespread of the free foods.

ROSE HIPS. For example, there is a familiar berry that, although you've maybe never sampled it, has the flavor of fresh apples. More important, its juice is from 6 to 24 times richer in Vitamin C than orange juice. Throughout much of the continent you can pick all you want the greater part of the year, even when temperatures fall a booming 60° below zero. As for recognizing this fruit, no one with a respect for brambles and a modicum of bush savvy is going to get the wrong thing by mistake. It is the rose hip, the ordinary seed pod of roses everywhere.

These rose hips have a delicate flavor that's delicious. They're free. They're strong medicine, to boot. Studies in Idaho found the scurvy-preventing vitamin in the raw pulp running from 4,000 to nearly 7,000 milligrams per pound. Daily human requirements, to give you a yardstick, are estimated to be 60 to 75 milligrams.

Three rose hips, the food experts say another way, have as much Vitamin C as an orange. We don't pay much attention to these gratuitous vitamins in the United States and Canada. But in England during World War II, some 5 mil-

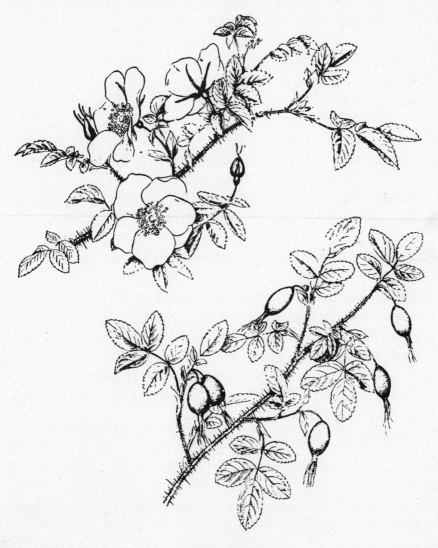

ROSE HIPS.

lion pounds of rose hips were gathered from the roadsides and put up to take the place of then scarce citrus fruits. Dried and powdered, rose hips are sold in Scandinavian countries for use in soups, for mixing with milk or water, to make hot and cold drinks, for sprinkling over cereals, etc., all of which they do admirably.

You get the good from this cousin of the apple, one of the many members of the rose family, whether you eat it off the bushes, cut up in salad, baked in cake or bannock, or boiled into jam or jelly. Matter of fact, plain dried rose hips are well worth carrying in a pocket for lunching on like raisins. To prepare them for this latter use, just cut each in half. Remove the central core of seeds. Dry the remaining shell-like skin and pulp quickly, as in a cool oven or in a kettle suspended above the fringes of a small campfire.

What I like to do with rose hips, when I catch my wife Vena in a cooking mood, is turn them into syrup. Snip the bud ends from a freshly gathered batch. Then cover the fruit with water and boil rapidly until soft. Strain off the juice. Return the pulp to the kettle, add enough water to cover, and make a second extraction. For every 2 cups of juice you end up with, add 1 cup of sugar. Boil until thick. Pour into sterilized bottles. That's all. Poured over steaming sourdough hotcakes blue-black winter mornings when the Northern Lights are still ablaze, this syrup never lasts us long.

Here's an extra hint. Don't throw away the pulp. Press it through a sieve to remove seeds and skins. Add half as much sugar as pulp. Put in clove, cinnamon, and any other spices or flavoring agents to taste. Heat covered until the sugar is dissolved. Then uncover and cook slowly until thick, stirring to prevent sticking. Pack in sterilized jars and seal. Voila! Fruit butter!

BERRIES. It's difficult to hunt or fish across a corner of North America, from the very deserts to the glittering ice cakes of the Arctic Ocean, that doesn't regularly yield wholesome and often delectable wild fruit. Until you count them, you may be surprised at how many you can name.

There are the numerous common grapes and cherries and

plums, the uniquely flavored little wintergreens, and there
are the crab apples that thrive wild from the southern states

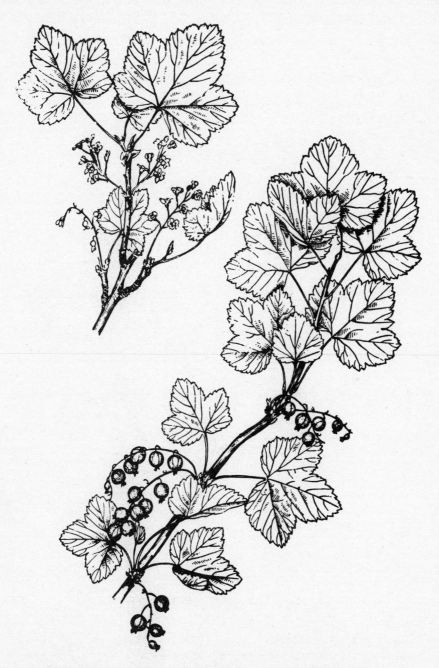

AMERICAN RED CURRANT. These spell jams, pies,
and jellies.

to the 49th State. There are the startlingly red but less familiar berries of the mountain ash that, crushed in water and sweetened, give a drink like lemonade. There are also the reddish-orange soapberries which, beaten with a little

AMERICAN RED RASPBERRY.

Even expert botanists have trouble trying to tell the numerous members of the raspberry family apart. Six are illustrated on this and following 3 pages. I don't bother, I just eat them.

sugar, foam into a salmon-colored froth that backwoodsmen still serve up as a pudding.

But there are the common blueberries, gooseberries, cranberries, and their ilk that every year fill out by the thousands of tons. And there are such other abounding members of the rose family as strawberries, blackberries, and raspberries— whose young stems and stalks are also tasty, and whose very leaves can be profitably steeped for tea.

THIMBLEBERRY.

TRAILING RASPBERRY.

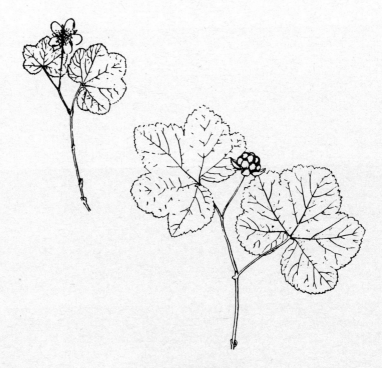

CLOUDBERRY.

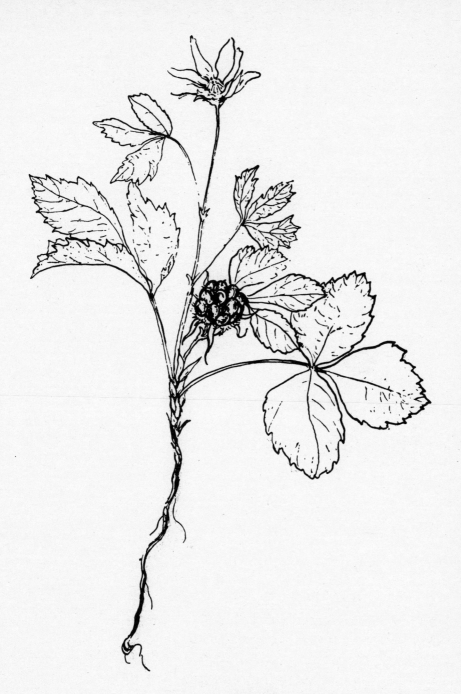

NAGOONBERRY.

SALMONBERRY.

PRICKLY PEAR. There's also the unlikely prickly pear. You don't know this one? Ever notice the little thorny knobs, ranging from the size of apricots to the size of large lemons, that bulge from the padlike joints of cactus? Those are the fellows. Actually, the spine-bristling skin of this fruit of the cactus is so unmistakable that any difficulties lie not in identifying but in picking. An easy way to go about this? With leather gloves and a knife.

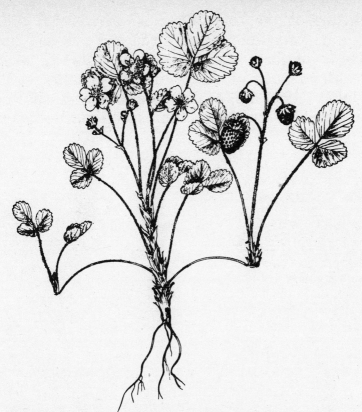

STRAWBERRY. Various forms of these are familiar everywhere.

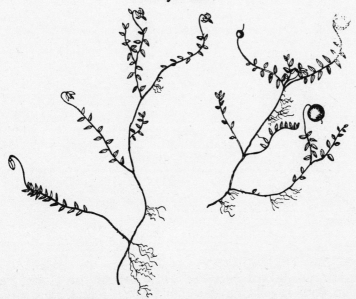

BOG CRANBERRY. Found in northern climes the world over, this member of the cranberry family is smaller than commercial varieties but is at least equally delicious.

Depending on the kind of cactus, the ripened colors of prickly pears vary from tawny green and purplish black to the choicest of them all—the big red fruits of the large *Opuntia Megacantha* of the continental Southwest. To eat any of these Indian figs, as they're also known, slice off the ends, slit the hide lengthways, and scoop out the pulp.

LOWBUSH CRANBERRY. Picked in the original 48 States and northward over the entire top of the globe, these cook up with sugar into delectable jams, jellies, and sauces.

BOG BLUEBERRY.

BARKS. Speaking of unlikely foods, there are forests of them. If in the back of your mind you figure that one day you may possibly be up against it for grub, perhaps because an accident to a companion keeps you in camp after your regular supplies are exhausted, it'll be reassuring to remember that the inner bark of the familiar birches is a historically important emergency food. You can eat it as is. The flavor, although sweetish, is also neutral enough to warrant its being added in chunks and strips to soups and mulligans. It retains its aromatic spiciness even when dried for easier packing.

As far as that goes, the lodgepole and other pines have an inner bark that is eatable both raw and cooked. A fishing crony of mine in the Yukon goes so far as to assert that this is at its finest when scraped from the south side of a young pine while the sap is rising. The poplar's sweetish sap layer, between the wood and the bitter outside bark, is also sustaining both raw and cooked.

You're not ordinarily going to bother doing it, but it may also be handy one day to know that dwindling flour stores have been augmented more than once with the dried and powdered inner barks of such trees as the poplar, birch, slippery elm, and the pines. I've eaten cakes made of straight lodgepole pine flour that was cooked, incidentally, with the white lard rendered from black bear fat. This breadstuff is dry and somewhat flat tasting. But it's an outdoor grub that will stand by you in a pinch. Realizing deep down that no matter what emergency overtakes you in the wilderness you're not likely to have to go hungry—well, I suppose that's one more reason why an individual gets to feel safe, secure, and never more relaxed than when out with rod, gun, or camping outfit in the primitive places.

GREENS. So you didn't think you knew at least a dozen wild eatables? If I were a wagering man, I'd be willing to lay odds that you've passed that dozen mark already. And we haven't even mentioned the wild lettuces, spinaches, and some of the other fine greens that are abundant nearly everywhere.

If you have ever sat down to a well prepared feed of wild vegetables, maybe you've noticed that they seem to taste better than domesticated varieties. I'll let you in on a trade secret. They are better.

Green leafy vegetables, to give just one example, deteriorate very quickly. Even when purchased as fresh as obtainable from the finest nearby market, they'll already have lost a sizeable proportion of vitamins. Some of the food values of greens diminish as much as one-third during the first hour after picking. But gather them fresh from nature's own garden and eat them while they're at their tastiest, and you'll enjoy the best they have to offer. It's a happy way to sharpen a satisfactory hunger, too.

LAMB'S-QUARTER. In a lot of hunting and fishing camps the acknowledged pick of the edible greens is lamb's-quarter. The tender tops of this wild spinach, which has none of the strong taste of market varieties, are delicious from early spring to frost-withering fall. The entire young plant is good from the ground up. Even from the older ones a quantity of tender leaves can usually be stripped. However, the pale green leaves with their mealy-appearing underneaths and the slim stalks are not the only taste-tempting compo-

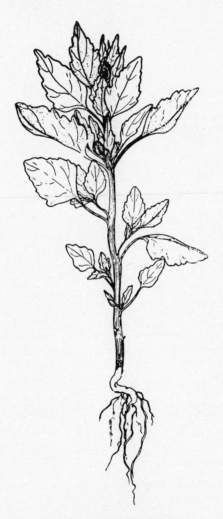

LAMB'S-QUARTER.

nents of this green, also widely known as pigweed and goose-
foot. Indians long used the ripe seeds for cereal and for grinding into meal. The tiny gleaming black discs, which develop
from elongated dense clusters of small green flowers, are
also handy for giving a pumpernickel complexion to camp
breads.

Along with other of the more tender leafy greens, lamb's-
quarter can be given a little more taste on occasion with the
help of a vinegar sauce. Such a flavorful acid also tends to

DANDELION.

preserve the vitamins in such vegetables. Alkalies, on the other hand, such as the commonly but inadvisedly used baking soda, destroy an unnecessary proportion of these food values.

For 4 cups of loosely packed greens, make with: 1 small onion, 4 slices bacon, ¼ cup vinegar, ¼ teaspoon salt, and pepper to taste. Shred the greens if they are large. Dice the onion. Mix. Then chop up the bacon and fry it until the bits become brown and brittle. Put in the vinegar, salt, and pepper and bring to a simmer. You now have two choices.

SEASHORE PLANTAIN. This representative of the plantain family, which is distributed throughout the world, finds favor whether used raw in salads or cooked like spinach.

You may pour the sauce over the raw greens. Or you may add the greens to the sauce and cook over low heat until they are limp. In either event, serve immediately.

PLANTAIN. Plantain is almost as good as lamb's-quarter. Furthermore, plantain is as well known to most of us as are the similarly prepared and eaten dandelions, although not usually by name. It is the short stemless potherb whose broadly elliptic green leaves rise directly from the root about a straight central spike. This singular spike blossoms, although you've possibly never noticed it, with minute greenish flowers that later turn into seeds. At any rate, you see plantain all over the world; even growing through sidewalks in New York, San Francisco, and Boston.

Plantain leaves make excellent greens. Fact is, the greener they are, the richer they are in Vitamins A and C and in minerals. Way I like them is boiled. What holds for plantain, when it comes to this common if often murderous method of cookery, goes for the other wild greens as well. Unless it means standing over a riled trail cook with a cleaver, try to see that all these are cooked only until just tender and still slightly crisp. This takes a surprisingly brief time. Even with such a formidable green as young nettles, which like prickly pears are best gathered with leather gloves and a knife, once the salted water has reached the boiling point and the dark green nettles have been dropped in, they'll be tender almost immediately and ready for that crowning pat of butter or margarine as soon as they're cool enough to eat.

The simple gimmick with these wild vegetables is to start them in a minimum amount of boiling water and to cook them, covered, as rapidly and briefly as possible. Young plantain and such can actually be lifted directly from the rinse to the saucepan and cooked without added water. For two liberal servings of slightly older greens, ½ cup water and ½ teaspoon salt will do the job. When the greens become tougher, a full cup of water may be required. Any of the vitamin-and-mineral-swarming fluid remaining should be used, as in soups, gravies, sauces and the like, unless there's some reason against this such as unusual bitterness. Me, I drink it.

WILD GREEN SOUP. Speaking of soups, though, here's a cream of wild green soup that really starts the mouth tingling; especially when you come in dehydrated from a day of hunting or fishing and get that first whiff of it, all

NETTLES.

GOOSETONGUE. Here is another of the plantains. Used like the rest, it is also sometimes canned for winter use.

steaming and savory. To go with 2 cups of chopped or scissored young mustard greens—or one of the other spicier greens such as dandelions, watercress, young wild radish tops, etc., if mustard isn't at hand—start slowly heating a quart of milk, not allowing it to boil.

Meanwhile, melt 2 tablespoons of butter, margarine, bacon drippings, or any other edible fat in a saucepan over low heat. Gradually stir in 1½ teaspoons salt, ⅛ teaspoon pepper, and 2 tablespoons flour. Add a finely minced small onion. Then pour in the hot milk bit by bit. Cook gently for 5 minutes. Drop in the greens and, stirring occasionally, continue to heat just below the boiling point until these are just tender. Sprinkle with paprika if you have any. Serve at once.

MUSTARD. Mustard, which flourishes wild over most of the globe, is universally recognizable because of its brilliant yellow flowers that become almost solid gold across many a field and hillside. This green, whether used in soup or elsewhere, is most agreeable when it first appears. The young stalks from which the leaves grow directly are not hard to identify, particularly as older mustard is often blooming in the same patch. These slightly peppery leaves are enjoyable raw. So are the young flowers with their then subtle pungency. The entire young plant goes well cooked with fish and game.

Even when you come upon wild mustard after it's grown old and tough, the easily gathered seeds are hard to equal for garnishing salads, adding to pickles and such for that extra seasoning, giving a final authority to barbecue sauces, and lending a wisp of zip and zest to venison mulligans. Mustard's very name comes from its seeds, being a corruption of *must-seeds* which harks back to ancient Roman-occupied Britain when these were processed by saturating them in a solution of grape juice or *must* as it was sometimes called.

Incidentally, table mustard can be made in camp by finely grinding wild mustard seeds, as between two stones, and adding enough water to make a paste. After that it's up to you. Commercially prepared condiments often contain such additional ingredients as vinegar, flour, salt, turmeric and other spices, and occasionally horseradish. This latter white-flowered member of the mustard family, with the pungent white roots, also grows wild.

FIREWEED. Fireweed, which in summer gives an unforgettable amethyst hue to vast fire-blackened stretches below some of my favorite sheep and goat ranges west of the Alaska Highway, is another wild vegetable difficult to mis-

FIREWEED. Young leaves, stems, and flowers are edible both raw and cooked. The young shoots, conspicuous because of red stems and bright green succulent leaves, are an asparagus substitute.

DWARF FIREWEED. Young leaves and stalks, mixed with a few buds for color and flavor, make fine salad and boiled greens. They all toughen and become increasingly bitter with age.

take. Thousands of square miles of burnt lands from the Aleutians and Greenland to Mexico soften to magenta annually, so showily do these tall perennials flame into spike-like clusters of flowers. Try cutting the young stems into sections and boiling them in a small amount of salted water until tender. This way they resemble asparagus. More mature stalks can be peeled and their sweetish interiors eaten raw. Young fireweed leaves cook up into satisfactory greens. But even if you can't get to these until fall, all is not lost. Steep them for tea.

HORSETAIL. Another wild green, notably simple to identify is the young horsetail. Nearly every fisherman and hunter has made his way through stands of this small green plant which prospers along corduroyed toteroads, about shaded brooks, and in other cool moist locations. Ever notice, when you've been relaxing on a log, how some of these give the impression of miniature pine forests? Others are reminiscent of whimsically dwarfed bamboos. The reason? The horsetail grows in two different forms.

The infertile horsetail has a single thin stem which resembles the trunk of a tiny pine all the more because of green shoots that branch out from it in a series of levels. The fertile horsetail thrusts upward in one bare stalk. This ascends in joints which a lot of us occasionally find ourselves pulling idly apart, section by popping section. The fertile horsetail is also known as the scouring rush; the gritty surfaces of the older plants make them handy articles to grab by the handful for scrubbing pans after an outdoor meal. As for eating, the outer tissues can be removed from the young shoots of both varieties and the somewhat sweetish interiors eaten raw.

OTHER WILD FOODS. In other words, there's no shortage of familiar wild vegetation that's good to eat. Plain ordinary clover, including both flowers and leaves, is a nutritious garnish for any salad. As for the sweet roots, try the Indian practice of dipping them in game drippings and then smoking them a bit over the smouldering outskirts of a campfire. Peeled young burdock stalks are another asparagus substitute. So are the upper parts of peeled young cattail shoots. Or shake the golden pollen from mature cattails and mix it half and half with the regular flour in pancake batters.

CATTAIL.

SPRING BEAUTY. The tender young leaves of this close relative of Miner's Lettuce can be added raw to salads or briefly cooked in a small amount of salted water for serving as a green vegetable.

Stems and leaves of the well-known miner's lettuce—whose clinching feature is the way a pair of leaves grow together part way up each short stem and form a cup through whose middle the stalk continues—are estimable salad fodder when young and a better-than-average spinach substitute when older.

As for kinnikinic, after you've filled up on the sustaining if blandly dry red berries, you can make yourself a smoke with the leaves. Dried and pulverized, these have been a frontier tobacco substitute for centuries.

Laziness in doing unnecessary things can be a great virtue. What I mean, one hungry outfit has only so much time and

KINNIKINIC.

energy. Why lug along a load of fresh vegetables and fruits on your outing if you can gather them fresher as you need them? A lot of time you'll do better to take instead enough other essentials to let you penetrate farther back of beyond, to where the big ones are holed up. A couple of good mottoes for most any vacationist to pin to his rucksack are: travel lighter, go farther. Pick instead of pack.

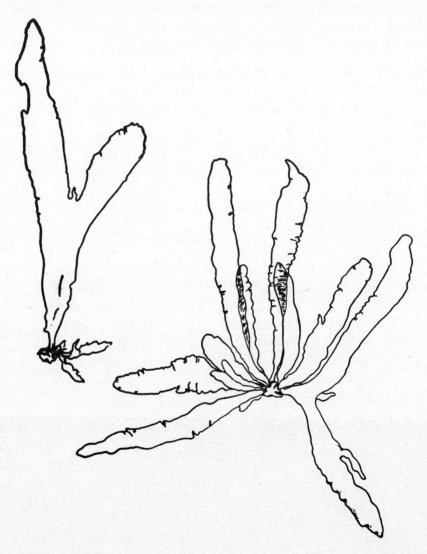

DULSE. This seaweed that grows attached to rocks is often added to soups and stews. It's also eaten fresh, a favorite method of preparation being to singe it quickly as by briefly dropping it into a hot frypan. Dulse is often **dried in the air and** stored for later use.

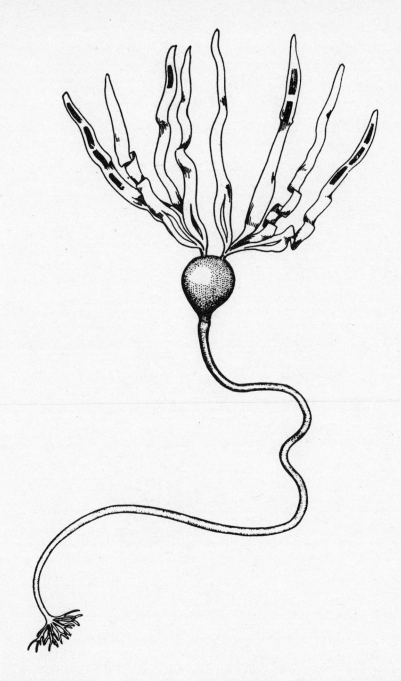

GIANT KELP. You can make pickles from these long
hollow stalks.

HIGHBUSH CRANBERRY. These have a distinctive sweetish sour odor and flavor which require a cultivated taste. However, they can get to be one of your favorite wild fruits. Frozen in winter, the berries melt pleasantly against the tongue like sherbet.

SALAL.   Want a taste treat? Try cooking up a few of these western wintergreen fruits in your applesauce. Indians dried them for winter feasting.

SERVICEBERRY. Also known as Juneberries, the numerous members of this family are used like the blueberries they resemble. Millions were once gathered to flavor pemmican.

WILD CUCUMBER. The tender young shoots are among my favorites in the spring because of the cucumberlike flavor they impart to salads. The oddly growing little berries are worth eating later.

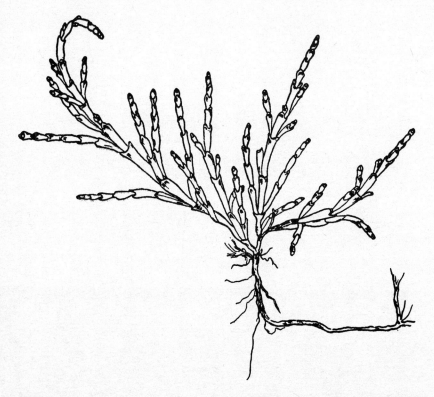

BEACH ASPARAGUS. Also known as Glasswort, this is often boiled as a potherb. However, it finds its main flavor when pickled. Very young plants blend especially well into salads predominated by oil and vinegar.

SOURDOCK. This member of the widespread dock family has tender young leaves that, more delicious because of an acid tang, make excellent salad greens as well as a fine cooked vegetable.

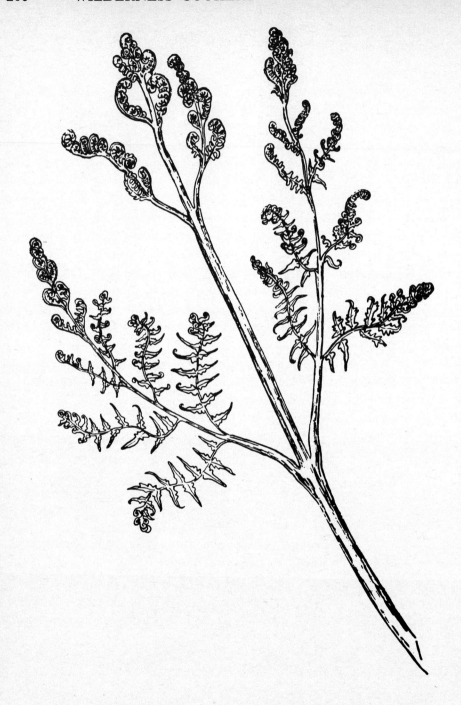

BRAKE. This is perhaps the most widely distributed and abundant of the ferns. The young fiddleheads, when some six to eight inches tall and still covered with a rusty scruffy material which is peeled off, are boiled and eaten like asparagus. They are not fit to eat when older.

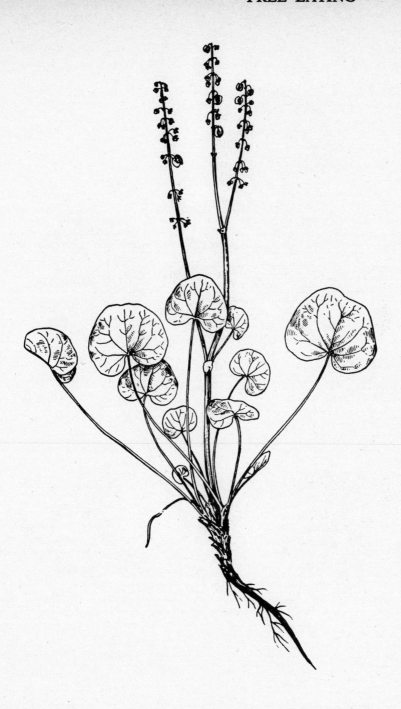

MOUNTAIN SORREL. The leaves of this member of the buckwheat family have a piquant acid taste that make them favorites for eating raw. The plant is also boiled as a green.

LABRADOR TEA. This evergreen's leaves, with their green tops and woolly underneaths, make an enjoyably aromatic tea when used in moderation. Another name is Hudson's Bay Tea. Two or three leaves are occasionally refreshing to chew raw.

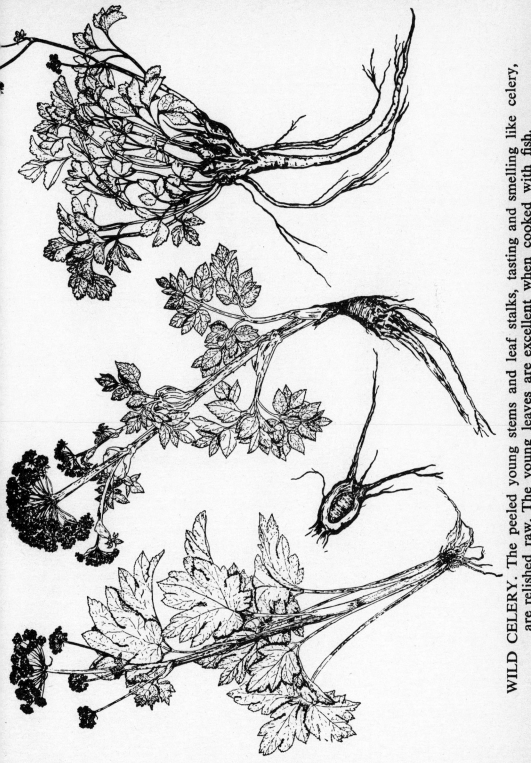

WILD CELERY. The peeled young stems and leaf stalks, tasting and smelling like celery, are relished raw. The young leaves are excellent when cooked with fish.

COWSLIP. The leaves, along with the thick hollow stems, should be boiled before flowers appear. (The leaves are not edible raw.) The buds become a delicacy when pickled in vinegar. Even the roots are good, looking like sauerkraut when they're boiled.

WINTERCRESS. This member of the mustard family is valued both as a salad green and as a potherb. The bitterness, found pleasant by many, increases with age and can be lessened by cooking in several changes of water.

CHAPTER 11

TOPPING IT OFF

ICE CREAM. Ice cream is one of the quickest and easiest of all desserts to make outdoors, especially after a fresh snow. Best for the purpose are dry flakes. You can also use the granular interior of the perpetual snowbanks found in the higher mountains, although the result will be more a coarse sherbet.

Just empty a can of evaporated milk into a large pot or bowl. A similar amount of dry milk, reconstituted with water, will do as well. Add 2 tablespoons of sugar, ⅛ teaspoon of salt, and some flavoring. Vanilla or one of the other extracts will serve. So will cocoa, powdered coffee, and the like. Mocha? Balance 2 teaspoons of powdered instant coffee with 1 teaspoon chocolate; enough, incidentally, for a quart of ice cream. If the flavoring, as for instance chocolate syrup, is already sweet, just omit the sugar.

Then quickly stir in fresh snow to taste. More sweetening and flavoring may be added at the end if you want. For this reason it is safest to go light on these initially. Otherwise, you'll have to repair any mistake with more milk and snow —not that this isn't a good excuse.

Three varieties that come out especially well, if you happen to like them to begin with, are the universally favored vanilla, rich dark chocolate with overtones of peppermint extract, and banana ice cream made with that particular extract.

TREELESS MAPLE SYRUP. The sugar maple grows only in North America. Like all green trees, it mysteriously changes water and carbon dioxide into sugar. So exceptional is the sugar maple's capacity for storing the sweet that this talent is a double boon. In autumn it produces some of the loveliest hues of the American forest; in spring, the amber succulence of maple syrup.

214

The only trouble many wilderness cooks have is that these latter activities are largely confined to such Eastern regions as the St. Lawrence Valley, New Brunswick and Nova Scotia, and such New England States as New Hampshire and Vermont. But there's a slightly incredible way around. You'll need: *Treeless Maple Syrup*

(6 medium potatoes
    2 cups water
    1 cup white sugar
    1 cup brown sugar

Peel the medium-sized potatoes. Boil uncovered with 2 cups water until but 1 cup of fluid remains. Remove the potatoes, for use any way you want. Stirring the liquid until the boiling point has again been reached, slowly add the sugar. Once this has entirely dissolved, set the pan off the heat to cool slowly. +

"Ghastly concoction," the old mountain man who gave me the formula nodded agreeably when, the initial time around, I first sampled the elixir at this primary stage. "Like home brew, it has to be aged in a dark place. After a couple of days in a bottle it'll be noble."

See if that first spoonful you doubtfully try doesn't seem to justify your worst suspicions, too. But bottle the syrup and tuck it away for several days to age. Taste it again at the end of that time and see if you, also, aren't pleasantly amazed.

HARD SAUCE. For hard sauce, cream ½ cup butter or margarine and gradually add 1½ cups of preferably powdered sugar. Beat until creamy. Toward the end add ½ teaspoon vanilla or some other flavoring.

CRANBERRY SAUCE. You frequently come across wild cranberries in the fall. Although smaller than domestic varieties, they are quickly picked. For a sauce that's particularly good with game, bring 1½ cups of water and 1 cup of sugar to a boil. After 10 minutes, drop 2 cups of washed cranberries into the syrup and let it continue to boil until the berries pop.

DRIED APPLES. These vary considerably. It will pay to buy the best obtainable, although outdoors most any dried apples taste delicious. Before using them, you'll ordinarily be best satisfied if you trim away any remaining portions of the core. Bruises should be cut out, too.

Brands differ, but on the average it takes about 7 pounds of fresh apples to make 1 pound of dried. Pressed into a measure, 1 pound of dehydrated apples contains some 4 cups of raw fruit. These cook up to roughly double bulk.

Applesauce, which may not get a second glance in the city, is relished in the open as a side dish with meat, as part of the stuffing for birds, atop cereal, and in numerous forms as a dessert. When the mercury threatens to shrink out of sight, try mixing some applesauce with evaporated milk and setting it in the cold, covered against the intrusion of small wild folk. The result will be a super ice cream, crystalline enough to eat easily.

Applesauce is handily enough made by simmering 2 cups of dried apples plus ⅛ teaspoon of salt in 4 cups of water until tender. If you want to go to the bother, press the cooked apples through a colander or such while they're hot. Stir 4 tablespoons of sugar and 1 teaspoon of nutmeg or cinnamon into the finished product, unless your palate dictates otherwise. Lemon or lemon juice, fresh or dehydrated, is also generally favored when available. Want something different? Coriander gives a piquant flavor. So does plain, everyday vanilla.

BAKED DRIED APPLES. Put 2 cups dried apples in an equal volume of boiling water. Set immediately off the heat and allow to stand 1 hour. Grease a shallow baking dish. Place the apples and liquid into this. Sprinkle with ½ teaspoon nutmeg, ½ teaspoon cinnamon, and 1 cup sugar. Slice ½ cup of margarine over the top.

Bake in a moderately hot oven or reflector baker ½ hour. Serve hot with milk. Or if you're where you can do it, mix up a quick batch of vanilla ice cream with the help of preferably light snow, as described elsewhere in this chapter, and put a few spoonfuls of that atop the hot apples.

APPLE CRUMB PUDDING. This takes on an even more pleasant campfire flavor if for the ½ cup of fat needed you mix bacon drippings with margarine or butter. Grease a baking dish with part of this. Put in 2 cups applesauce. Rub together ¾ cup of preferably brown sugar and an equal volume of flour with the remaining fat until crumbly. Spread this over the apples and bake everything in a hot oven or reflector baker 15 minutes.

APPLE APPEALS. Make enough bannock biscuits to go around, according to the directions in the chapter on bread. Top each—after the bottom crust has formed and the bannock has been turned if it is being cooked atop the heat; at once if the bannock will not have to be turned— with slices of dried apple that have been brought to a simmer in just enough water to cover and then allowed to cool in their own juice. Over these spread thin yellow slices of tangy cheese. A dutch oven, reflector baker, or regular oven is best for preparing this dessert.

STEWED PRUNES. Cover the prunes with cold water, bring to a bubble, and keep barely simmering until the fruit is soft.

Or let the prunes plump up overnight in enough water to cover. Cook slowly in the same fluid until done to your taste. Then add sugar if you like. Some also like to include lemon. Sometime when you want a particularly delectable syrup, try soaking and cooking the prunes in strong black tea. You won't be able to detect the tea taste, by the way. A little cinnamon and lemon will improve even this singular flavor.

PRUNE BREAD. Soak a pound of prunes in cold water until they are juicy and plump. Then remove them, take out the pits, if any, and cut or chop the fruit into small bits. Cover with 1½ cups boiling water. You'll also need:

> 2½ cups sifted flour
> 1½ cups sugar
> 1 teaspoon cinnamon
> 1 teaspoon salt
> 2½ teaspoons baking soda
> 2 eggs
> ½ cup melted shortening

Sift or mix together the flour, sugar, cinnamon, salt, and baking soda. Add the prunes and water. Beat the eggs or stir together the equivalent amount of dried eggs and water. Mix these, then the shortening, into the other ingredients. Pour into a greased bread pan and bake in a moderately slow oven or reflector baker for 1 hour or until done. Remove from the pan and cool.

STEWED APRICOTS. Cover the dried apricots with cold water. Bring this to a dancing boil for 15 minutes or until the fruit is tender. Another way is to cover the apricots with hot water, set them away from the heat for 2 hours or so, and then simmer slowly in the same water until soft. During the final few minutes of cooking, add sugar to taste if you care for any additional sweetening. I don't.

DRIED APRICOT COBBLER. We used to get cobblers a lot back at century-and-a-half-old Kimball Union Academy in Meriden, New Hampshire. Essentially, as you know, these are deep-dish New England fruit pies, aptly flung together in a hurry and unerringly topped with a biscuit mixture. In the woods you can bake these practically by ear, using both wild and dried fruits. Here is a basic recipe featuring dried apricots:

> 2 cups dried apricots
> ½ cup sugar
> 1 cup water
> 3 tablespoons lemon juice
> 3 tablespoons margarine
> ½ teaspoon cinnamon
> 3 tablespoons sugar

Wash the apricots and cut into pieces. Cover with water and cook until tender. Add the sugar when almost done. Transfer the hot fruit to a baking dish or casserole and add lemon juice if available. Dot with margarine. Sprinkle with cinnamon and the remaining 3 tablespoons of sugar.

Spoon soft biscuit dough over the fruit. Cut vents to allow steam to escape. Bake in hot oven or reflector baker about 30 minutes or until crust is done. Serve hot with whipped evaporated milk, vanilla ice cream, etc.

For the crust:

> 1 cup sifted flour
> 1 tablespoon sugar

    1 teaspoon baking powder
    ½ teaspoon salt
    2 tablespoons shortening
    ½ cup milk

Mix the flour, sugar, baking powder, and salt. Cut in the shortening. Have everything ready to go. Then quickly stir in enough milk to make a soft dough. Spoon this dough immediately atop the fruit and get the whole thing into the preheated oven without delay.

DRIED FRUIT TURNOVERS. A blend of dried apricots and prunes is good for these turnovers, although numerous other such combinations are pleasing, whether devoured hot from the fire or eaten cold for lunch. Simmer a heaping cup apiece of apricots and pitted prunes with 1½ cups of water until the fruit begins to come apart. Then stir in 1 cup sugar, 1 tablespoon flour, ½ teaspoon nutmeg, and 5 tablespoons margarine.

Make the pastry by creaming ½ cup of butter or margarine, then mixing in 1 cup flour and 2 tablespoons water. Roll into a sheet. Cut out 8 ovals about the size of a saucer. Fill each with fruit, fold over, press the edges together, and prick the tops with a fork to make a vent for steam. Bake in a moderately slow oven or reflector baker until tan and crisp.

PEACH SHORTBREAD.
    3 cups quick-cooking oats
    ½ cup sugar
    ¼ cup flour
    ¼ teaspoon salt
    ¾ cup margarine
    1 teaspoon vanilla extract
    stewed dried peaches

Mix the dry ingredients. Cut in the margarine. Finally, stir in the vanilla extract. Press across the bottom of a greased oven pan. Put in a preheated moderately warm reflector baker or oven and bake 1½ hours or until lightly browned. Cut or break into chunks. Drench with stewed dried peaches.

BERRIES AND DUMPLINGS. This is a cinch when you

camp in blueberry, raspberry, blackberry, strawberry, saskatoon, and other berry country. Just pick enough berries for dessert. Stew them over the campfire, sweetening them the way you like them. When you're ready to sit down to the main meal, drop on a white dome of dumplings. Cover the pot tightly.

When the dumplings are done, take out and top each with a spoonful of margarine. Spoon the hot berries over them. Pour on some milk if you want. And see what everyone's idea is about the dessert for the following meal.

STRAWBERRY SHORTCAKE. All you need for this tiptop treat is wild strawberries and hot bannock. To match about 2 quarts of berries, freshly picked and left standing drenched with a cup of sugar, here's one way to go about the latter:

> 2 cups sifted flour
> 2 tablespoons sugar
> 2 teaspoons baking powder
> 1 teaspoon salt
> 4 tablespoons shortening
> ½ cup cold milk (or more)

The first time I ever ate this one was on Ottertail Creek, in the middle of the Canadian Rockies, with trapper and riverman Billy Kruger doing the cooking. We'd run out of lard a week earlier. Instead, Billy used some oil he'd previously rendered from a couple of young grizzlies.

Billy Kruger commenced the rites by sifting all the dry ingredients together into a bowl. He worked in the shortening, then stirred in enough cold milk to make a soft dough.

This dough Billy kneaded very briefly on a floured board. Using a clean cold bottle, he rolled it out about ½ inch thick. Half of the dough he laid in a greased pan and dotted with chunks of canned butter. The other half he spread on top. If you prefer individual biscuits, just cut the dough into ovals with a floured can top or glass. Baking in a very hot oven or reflector baker takes 12 to 15 minutes.

Afterwards we carefully separated the steaming layers, ladled the sweetened berries between and above, and fell to it. Raspberries, blueberries, saskatoons, blackberries, and similar wild fruits are also good with this hot bannock.

WHIPPED CREAM. That particular summer evening we crowned the shortcake with whipped cream made from evaporated milk. There's a simple gimmick to this. Milk and utensils have to be icy cold. This we arranged easily enough by submerging bowl, beater, and can of milk in the mountain stream that sparkled past Billy Kruger's cabin on its way to mingle with the Peace River.

So chilled, most evaporated milk quickly whips to about triple volume. A couple of tablespoons of lemon juice can be used to increase the stiffness after the milk is partially whipped. Some bush cooks also use an envelope (1 tablespoon) of unflavored gelatin, dissolved in a minimum of water, for this purpose.

FRIED WILD STRAWBERRIES. Clean 4 cups of fresh strawberries except for their stems. Chill the berries as much as possible, perhaps by partly immersing their container in a brook or spring. Keep the berries dry.

For the batter, beat 1 egg with 1 cup of milk. Then add 1 tablespoon melted margarine, ⅛ teaspoon salt, ¼ cup sugar, and 1 teaspoon vanilla. Blend thoroughly. Mix 1½ cups flour with 3 teaspoons baking powder. Combine with the egg mixture and beat until smooth.

Hold each chilled berry by its stem and dip carefully into the batter. Then drop into hot deep fat and fry until well browned. This will take about a minute. Save what you don't eat on the spot to mete out with whipped cream for dessert.

OPEN STRAWBERRY PIE. To make a 9-inch pie shell, sift together 1 cup of sifted flour and ½ teaspoon salt. Cut in ½ cup of shortening. For the flakiest and tastiest pie crust, use rendered bear grease.

Handling the crust quickly and lightly, add only enough water, about 3 teaspoons, to make a dough that will hold together when rolled. Roll out and spread on a greased pie pan. Bake in a hot oven or reflector baker for 12 to 15 minutes or until done.

Simmer together 1 cup of crushed wild strawberries, ½

cup sugar, and 2 tablespoons of cornstarch until they've become thick and syrupy. Meanwhile, pack the cooked pie shell with the ripest and juiciest strawberries you have. Drench them with the hot strawberry syrup. Chill and serve.

This pie is delicious, too, when similarly prepared with raspberries, thimbleberries, blackberries, and such. Sweetening may be varied to taste.

APPLE PIE. Make enough pastry for a 2-crust pie. If you don't already have a favorite recipe for pastry, the one with the strawberry pie is a good one. Roll out thin and line a deep 9-inch pie pan or plate, heavily greased with margarine.

cooked dried apples, chopped
1 cup sugar
½ teaspoon nutmeg
4 teaspoons flour
4 tablespoons corn syrup
¼ pound margarine

Dot the lower pie shell, once it is in the pan, with half the margarine, sliced thin. Mix the sugar, nutmeg, and flour. Sprinkle half of it over the bits of margarine. Heap the pie tin full of chopped cooked apples and pour the corn syrup among them. Sprinkle on the remaining sugar, nutmeg, and flour.

Fold on the top layer of pastry. Cut a pinetree of vents in the middle of the top crust to allow steam to escape. Slice the other half of the margarine over it. Bake in a preheated hot oven or reflector baker for 40 to 50 minutes or until the crust is done.

The uneven heat that a lot of outdoor cooking contraptions put out gives trouble sometimes by overcooking the rims of pies. One solution is to overturn the empty pie plate on a sheet of aluminum foil, maybe before you leave home. Draw a line ½ inch beyond the edge of the pan. Take away the pan and draw a second circle 1½ inches inside the first. Cut out this foil crust-protector with scissors. Laid over the fluted edges of the pie, it will shield the dough from overbrowning.

DRIED APRICOT PIE.

> 3 cups cooked, unsweetened apricots, drained
> ½ cup apricot juice
> 1 tablespoon cornstarch
> ½ cup sugar
> ⅛ teaspoon salt
> 1 tablespoon margarine

Drain the cooked, unsweetened apricots. Combine ½ cup of the juice from the cooked fruit with the cornstarch, sugar, and salt. Cook and stir until thick and clear. Remove from stove and melt in the margarine.

Arrange the apricots in a pastry-lined 9-inch pie pan. Pour the juice mixture over them. Top with pastry strips. Bake in a hot oven or reflector baker for about 30 minutes or until the pastry is done. This is really a treat when big wet flakes begin tumbling thickly among the pines.

GOOSEBERRY PIE. Double-crust gooseberry pie was famous back in colonial days. Just blend 3 cups of fresh ripe gooseberries, 1 cup of brown sugar, and 2 tablespoons of flour. The crust story is the same. Bake in a hot oven or reflector baker for 15 minutes to seal the crust and deter any running over. Then lower the heat to moderate and bake for 35 to 40 minutes more or until the pastry is brown on top.

BLUEBERRY PIE. This pie isn't so solid with thickeners such as arrowroot, tapioca, or cornstarch that it will hold stolidly together while you punctuate your conversation with the occasional forkful. As a matter of fact, most campers who sit down to this particular dessert are glad to hold up on the repartee for awhile and to finish off with a spoon.

All you need besides the pastry is 4 cups of fresh blueberries, 1 cup sugar, and ¼ cup of melted margarine. As for the cooking, it takes place in a single operation.

Line a greased pie pan with pastry. Mix the berries, sugar, and margarine. Pour them into the uncooked shell. Top with the upper crust, being sure to cut vents. Bake in a preheated, moderately hot oven or reflector baker about 50 minutes or until the crust is golden tan.

BLUEBERRY SLUMP. Bring 4 cups blueberries, 1½

cups sugar, 4 tablespoons cornstarch, and 1 teaspoon nutmeg slowly to a boil in a heavy saucepan. While the mixture is simmering, make a batter of:

> 4 tablespoons sugar
> 3 tablespoons shortening
> ½ cup milk
> 1½ cups sifted flour
> 1½ teaspoons baking powder
> ¼ teaspoon salt

Cream the sugar and shortening. Add the milk and blend thoroughly. Mix the flour, baking powder, and salt. Stir rapidly into the other ingredients.

Then begin dropping the batter, spoonful by spoonful, over the bubbling berries. Cover and cook at the same speed for 10 minutes. Serve hot with cream, if you have it, or with vanilla ice cream if there's snow for quickly stirring together a bowlful.

RASPBERRY SLUMP. Here is a variation of Blueberry Slump adjusted to raspberries. This recipe can also be used for prunes, dried peaches, blackberries, etc. by gearing the sugar and spices by taste to the natural flavor of the fruit.

> 1 cup sugar
> 1 tablespoon cornstarch
> 1 cup boiling water
> 3 cups raspberries
> 1 tablespoon margarine
> ½ teaspoon cloves
> ½ teaspoon cinnamon

Mix the sugar and cornstarch in a pan. Slowly add the boiling water and, continually stirring, bring to a simmer for a minute. Add the raspberries to the syrup. While the mixture is bubbling, proceed as in the preceding Blueberry Slump recipe.

CITRUS FRUIT PEEL. Oranges, grapefruit, lemons, and other citrus fruits are so much trouble to come by in many parts of the wilderness that when you get any, you may as well utilize them to the fullest possible degree. Instead of throwing away the skins as you would in the city, why not make candied peel?

Peel can be kept until you accumulate enough to bother with by immersing it in salt water. This will also remove some of the bitter taste. The skins should then be well rinsed in fresh water, boiled until tender, cut into bite-size bits, and slowly simmered in a thick sugar syrup until transparent. Drain as in a coarse sieve. Cool on a plate. Then roll in either powdered or granulated sugar.

Or if the fruit is eaten quickly, just gather the dry peel. If you want to cut down on any later bitterness, which on the other hand many relish, remove some of the white underneath of the skin with a spoon. Cut the peel into strips, perhaps with scissors. Put the peel from a dozen oranges, for example, in a saucepan along with 1½ cups water and 3 cups sugar. Simmer slowly until clear. Then proceed as above.

For something a little different, candied peel may be dipped in melted chocolate. Adding one of the instant coffees to the chocolate in proportions of 2 to 1 will give you a mocha flavor. Lay on paper to cool and dry.

SOURDOUGH CAKE. Sourdough (see chapter on breads) is still on the job those blusterous, rainy days when the masculine cook's mind turns to such possibilities as camp cake. Here's the way with that old stand-by, chocolate:

1	cup thick sourdough starter
1	cup water
1½	cups flour
¼	cup dry skim milk

Mix. Allow to ferment for several hours near the warmth until light and bubbly. Then in a separate pan blend:

2	cups sugar
½	cup shortening
4	squares bitter chocolate
2	eggs
1	teaspoon vanilla
½	teaspoon salt
1½	teaspoons baking soda

Rub and stir the sugar and shortening together until fluffy. Melt the chocolate and add that.

If using whole eggs, separate the whites and yolks. Beat

the yolks. Add the vanilla, then the salt and soda. Mix thoroughly with the sugar, shortening, and chocolate. Or just mix reconstituted dehydrated eggs, vanilla, salt, and soda, and add these. In either case, blend this second combination with the sourdough. If the egg whites are separate, now beat them stiff and fold them into the batter.

Pour into a large greased pan. Bake in moderate heat for 25 to 30 minutes or until done.

Cool. Then, if you want, ice with your choice of frosting. For a clear brown caramel coating, for instance, just stir a cup of sugar in a heavy frypan over moderate heat. When the sugar melts, spread it over the cake with a hot table knife.

TOMATO SOUP CAKE. Cream 2 tablespoons of shortening with 1 cup sugar. Add 1 well beaten egg. Sift together 2 cups flour, 1 teaspoon cloves, ½ teaspoon mace, ½ teaspoon nutmeg, ½ teaspoon baking soda, and 3 teaspoons baking powder. Stir these into the above, along with 1 can of condensed tomato soup. Add 1 cup seeded raisins, lightly floured.

Pour the batter into a small greased pan. Bake in a moderate oven 1 hour or until done. And unless you're an old hand with this sort of thing, be ready to be rather pleasantly surprised.

INDIAN PUDDING. Before Columbus and his cohorts mistakenly reached this continent while en route somewhere else, the rest of the world had never heard of redskins, corn, nor of course of Indian Pudding. The latter has done well to retain its distinctive name so long, during which time a native American bird has been dubbed a turkey and another equally American vegetable has achieved fame, even here, as the Irish potato.

Indian Pudding is something we like, particularly about the time of the first autumn snowfall when you can manufacture a bowl full of vanilla ice cream in about 5 minutes flat. It's also something in the mountains in summer, up by the snow line, although then the secondary enrichment you have to settle for is a more pebbly sherbet.

Scald 4 cups of whole milk in a double boiler. Gradually

stir in 5 tablespoons of corn meal and cook 15 minutes, constantly stirring. Then add: 2 tablespoons of margarine, ½ teaspoon salt, ¼ teaspoon nutmeg, ½ teaspoon cinnamon, ½ teaspoon ginger, 2 well beaten or well mixed eggs, and 1 cup molasses. Turn into a greased baking dish, pour on 1 cup of cold milk, and bake in a slow oven or reflector baker 1½ hours.

H.B.C. PLUM PUDDING. If you're going to be hunting in the bush with a friend or two on Thanksgiving and want to have something a little special for that occasion, you may be interested in going prepared to make one of the aromatic Hudson's Bay Company puddings which—traditionally varying in accordance to what ingredients have been at hand—have crowned many a holiday feast in the silent places since the Company was founded May 2, 1670.

The following components can be mixed at home and sealed in a plastic container:

4	cups sifted flour
4	teaspoons baking powder
½	teaspoon cinnamon
½	teaspoon nutmeg
1	cup brown sugar
½	cup white sugar
¼	cup finely chopped glaceed fruit mix
2	cups seedless raisins
1	cup currants
4	tablespoons dehydrated whole egg
6	tablespoons dehydrated whole milk
¼	teaspoon powdered lemon juice

When the memorable day arrives, shake and stir all these ingredients together, along with 2 cups finely minced suet. This can be either beef suet brought for the occasion or animal suet obtained on the spot. Add 2 cups water to make a cake batter. You will have also packed along a heavy cotton bag, and this you will have just wrung out in hot water and sprinkled inside with flour. Pour the batter into this. Tie the top tightly, leaving plenty of room for expansion.

Place this immediately in a pot filled with sufficient boiling water to cover. Keep it boiling 3 hours, turning the bag upside down when the pudding starts to harden so that all the fruit will not settle to the bottom. As the cooking continues, shift the bag occasionally so it will not scorch against the sides of the receptacle. At the end, dip this cloth container briefly in cold water and carefully remove the fabric so as not to break or crumble the pudding.

Serve this plum pudding hot with some appropriate sauce. Butter and sugar, flavored with some spice such as nutmeg or an extract such as lemon powder, will suffice. So will the thick juice from boiled dehydrated fruit.

Every time I enjoy one of these in the bush, I think of Voltaire acidly describing the North two centuries ago as "A patch of snow inhabited by barbarians, bear, and beaver." He should have seen the top of this continent when it's in a holiday mood.

CHAPTER 12

POTPOURRI

BAKING TEMPERATURES. If space and weight are no problems, one thing to do while accumulating experience is to bring along a small oven thermometer unless such is already attached to your cooking contraption. One costs only a few cents, occupies very little room, and takes much of the initial guesswork out of baking with outdoor fires. The following table will then apply; all temperatures mentioned in this book being the commonly used Fahrenheit, whereby at sea level fresh water freezes at 32° and boils at 212°.

Slow oven	250° to 325°
Moderate oven	325° to 400°
Hot oven	400° to 450°
Very hot oven	450° to 550°

If you're starting out with no such thermometer, you will be able to get a fairly accurate idea of the temperature by using the following test. With experience, of course, you'll be able to make the same approximations by holding the bare hand in the heat. In the meantime, sprinkle some white flour in a pan and place this in the heated oven or baker. If you're short on flour, a piece of white tissue paper can be used instead.

Turns light tan in 5 minutes	Slow Oven
Turns medium golden tan in 5 minutes	
	Moderate Oven
Turns deep dark brown in 5 minutes	Hot Oven
Turns deep dark brown in 3 minutes	
	Very Hot Oven

FOOD AT HIGH ALTITUDES. When pioneers first pushed their way westward into Rocky Mountain country, they had trouble for a time in successfully boiling such staples as vegetables and meats, while favorite bannock and oc-

229

casional family cake recipes turned out to be dismaying failures.

The difference in atmospheric pressures was, and still is, the cause of such difficulties. Just as the pressure of water is greatest at the bottom of the sea and lightest just below the surface, so it is in the ocean of atmosphere in which we live. The pressure of the air is greatest below and at sea level. It becomes comparatively less the higher we climb.

Water, being under less pressure the loftier the altitude, boils at lower and lower temperatures the higher we go. This means that foods boiled or simmered at higher altitudes require a correspondingly longer cooking time. There are so many variations in foods themselves that it is difficult to give any definite rules. In general, such cooking times must be increased from 4 to 11 percent per 1,000 feet above sea level. Until you've had experience with a particular food, a safe rule is to add roughly 10 percent per 1,000 feet. A few minutes before that time is reached, start testing or tasting.

MOUNTAIN CAKES. Cake recipes may be modified by using the following table. Results vary with different types of cake, however, so the following data can be no more than a general guide:

Baking powder
3,000 to 4,000 feet
          Use ⅞ teaspoon for every cup flour
4,000 to 6,000 feet
          Use ¾ teaspoon for every cup flour
6,000 feet and above
          Use ½ teaspoon for every cup flour

Sugar
For rich cakes which contain ½ cup or more of fat and over 1 cup of sugar per 2 cups of flour, decrease the sugar ½ tablespoon for every 1,000 feet rise in elevation above sea level. Lean cakes containing less fat and less sugar than above do not need this sugar correction.

Liquid
At high altitudes, cakes tend to be more dry. In-

creasing the liquid ½ to 1 tablespoon results in a more moist and less crumbly product.

MILE-HIGH BREADS. With bannock and similar bread-stuffs: up to 5,000 feet, use 1 teaspoon of double action baking powder for every cup of flour as suggested elsewhere in this book. At 7,500 feet, decrease this to ¾ teaspoon baking powder. At 10,000 feet, use only ½ teaspoon of baking powder. Other ingredients remain the same. Follow the recipe for the nearest altitude.

At high altitudes, sourdough and other yeast bread should be allowed to rise for a shorter time, only until about doubled in bulk. Either that, or less leavening should be used. The first technique assures better results.

Because flour dries out faster at high altitudes, it may be necessary to use more liquid to compensate for this loss and to give the dough the desirable consistency.

WATER. Water from springs and streams that flow from clean and uninhabited North American country is usually safe for drinking and cooking. In the wilderness lake regions of northern United States and Canada, the water from these bodies, unless there are many camps on the shores or along the courses running into them, is also generally pure. This does not always hold true, however. Even if it did, we are not always familiar enough with a region to know the condition of a watershed a short distance away.

When we have the slightest doubt about whether or not water is pure, it should be treated as though unsafe. This includes not only the water we drink. It also involves the water used for cooking and for washing.

Cooking and eating implements that have been washed in contaminated water can carry disease germs even though the cooking water is pure or is boiled in the process of cooking. In some localities, uncooked vegetables such as lettuce and radishes are unsafe. Water can often be cleared by letting it seep into a hole dug a few feet from a shore, but such filtration does not assure purity.

PURIFYING WATER. The easiest and most practical way to sterilize doubtful water is to boil it. At or near sea level, hard boiling for five minutes will do the job. For every additional 1,000 feet altitude, a safe all-around pre-caution is to increase the boiling time one minute.

Or you can use halazone tablets which may be secured at most sporting goods stores. A small two-ounce bottle containing 100 tablets costs about 50 cents and takes up less room than a 12-gauge shell. Because this process depends on the release of chlorine gas, the tablets should be fresh and the container kept tightly closed. Dissolve one tablet in a quart of water and let it stand for ½ hour. If the water is murky or particularly doubtful, both the time and the number of tablets may well be doubled. Slosh a little of this water over the lips of the container after the first few minutes to sterilize these. Then cover the receptacle as tightly as possible.

In Mexico and other semitropical and tropical regions, chlorine-releasing compounds can not be depended upon. Water there should either be boiled or, when this is not convenient, treated with Iodine Water Purification Tablets.

ICE. Ice is no more pure than was the water from which it was frozen. Although heat destroys bacteria and parasites, cold very definitely does not.

COOLING WATER. In warm country, water may be chilled without ice to a palatable temperature by the use of water-cooling bags. These commonly hold up to several gallons and are slightly porous so that a little fluid continues to seep out and to wet the outside. This exterior moisture evaporates in the air and so lowers the interior temperature. The process may be quickened by hanging the bag in a breeze. This water you can purify at the same time by dropping in the necessary tablets.

SNOW. The only precaution that need be taken with pure snow in the wilderness is to treat it like ice cream and not put down too much at once while overheated or chilled. Aside from that, clean snow can be safely eaten any time you are thirsty in the bush.

Wilderness snows, after all, afford in flake form the purest of distilled water obtainable from the atmosphere. Snow's primary drawback is that a considerable amount is required to obtain the desired quantity of water. You soon

WATER-COOLING BAG.

learn to break off sections of any available crust. Heavy granular snow from former storms, you find, is usually more convenient still.

This lower water content is quickly evident the first time you melt snow in the noon tea pail. Particular care has to be taken not to burn the utensil, particularly as snow also acts as a blotter. This is a reason why a few mouthfuls seem actually parching. The safest technique when you want to boil the kettle is to melt snow in small quantities until the bottom of the container is protected with several inches of water. You can then begin filling it with more and more snow until the required amount of liquid is obtained.

These shortcomings are more than compensated for by the fact that snowfall makes water readily available throughout the woods, mountains, plains, and deserts it whitens. All one has to do is scoop up clean handfuls while walking along. The body requires considerably more water in cold weather than most of us would ordinarily expect. For one thing, the kidneys then have to take over part of the process of elimination otherwise accomplished by the perspiration glands. For another thing, the comparative dryness of the air increases the amount of body water removed from respiratory passages. The immediate results if such water is not reasonably replaced? Listlessness and fatigue! Snow used in place of drinking water, far from being harmful or dangerous, is therefore an extremely healthful convenience.

DISH WASHING. Washing dishes is not really much of a chore if you have some system about it and if you always clean up immediately after a meal. With your cook kit, you'll find it helpful to include such items as detergent, two small tough cellulose sponges or dish cloths, a little dish mop for that hot campfire water, and scouring pads that combine steel wool or such with soap.

While you are eating, have your largest kettle over the fire heating dishwater. Or at the jumping-off spot, perhaps, buy a cheap tin dishpan if you've the room and ditch it when the trip is over. This will not take up much space if you select a model into which other items in your outfit can nest.

If you prefer, you may take along a small canvas wash basin. Such a 7-ounce affair that I've carried on go-light trips for years is 4 inches high and 12 inches in diameter. It squashes down flat to pack.

Every camper, as he finishes his meal, scrapes his prob-

CANVAS WASH BASIN.

ably nearly clean plate into the fire. When you are through with the frypans, pour off all grease and wipe them clean. Then fill them with water and put them on the fire to boil. Do the same with any kettle containing the sticky residue of mush.

Down at the creek or lake shore you will find clusters of grass or other vegetation such as scouring rushes, with mud or sand adhering to the roots. Pull up a clump and use it to scour the outside of pots and also both the interior and exterior of the frypans before you wash them. Pans in which cereals like rolled oats have been cooked are particularly bothersome. If you will put a little square of butter or oleomargarine in the water when you are preparing the cereal, it will make the pot ten times easier to clean.

If you have a pet aluminum pot whose exterior you want to keep bright, coat the outside with a film of soap before you place it on the fire. All trace of black will then quickly wash off. Eventually, most kettles get thoroughly darkened on the outside with soot which sticks most tenaciously and which can scarcely be removed by anything short of abrasives. But this soot does no harm whatever and even makes food in such a kettle cook faster and more evenly. If you scour with sand or with muddy vegetation, very little will rub off on other things when you pack. It is customary to have a canvas bag in which to stow the nest of pans and kettles. This helps to keep them from blackening other articles in the outfit. Individual fabric containers may also be convenient.

It has been the experience of a great many of the old sourdoughs in Alaska and the Northwest that when a utensil used for cooking meat is washed with soap, they get bad digestive disturbances akin to poisoning and that this ceases when such washing is stopped. One way to clean a steel frypan is to heat it very hot, then quickly plunge it into cold water. If this does not remove all the dirt, then scrub with sand and rinse in clear boiling water. Another way of loosening grease is to fill the pan with water into which some wood ashes have been dropped and allow the whole thing to come to a boil beside the blaze.

OUTDOOR COOKING TERMS

Bake   To cook by dry heat, as in a reflector baker or oven.

Baste   To moisten cooking food with melted fat, drippings, or other liquid.

Boil   To cook in water, or liquid mostly water, at boiling temperature (212° F. at sea level). Bubbles rise continually and break on the surface.

Braise   To brown in fat, then cook in covered pan, with or without added liquid, over fire, in reflector baker, dutch oven or other oven. Larger pieces of meat cooked by braising are called pot roasts.

Broil   To cook uncovered by direct heat over an open fire.

Deep-fry   See french-fry.

French-fry To cook in a deep receptacle, in enough hot fat to cover or float food.

Fricassee	To braise individual serving pieces of meat, poultry, or game in a little liquid—water, broth, or sauce.
Fry	To cook in fat.
Grill	See broil.
Marinate	To let foods stand in a liquid (usually mixture of oil with vinegar or lemon juice) to add flavor or make more tender.
Pan-broil	To cook in very lightly greased or ungreased heavy pan on top of stove. Any fat is poured off as it accumulates so food does not fry.
Pan-fry	See saute.
Parboil	To boil until partly cooked.
Plank	To cook and serve on wooden slab or board.
Poach	To cook under the boiling point covered in hot liquid.
Pot-roast	See braise.
Render	To free fat from connective tissue by slowly heating until fat melts and can be poured off.
Roast	To bake in hot air, in reflector baker or turning over open fire, without water or cover.
Saute	To cook in a small amount of fat.
Scald	To heat to a temperature just below the boiling point.
Sear	To seal surface by exposing it to intense heat.
Simmer	To cook in liquid just below the boiling point. Bubbles form slowly and break below the surface.
Skewer	To pierce with pointed stick.
Steam	To cook food in steam over boiling water. Food is steamed in a covered container, on a rack or in a perforated pan above boiling water.
Steep	To extract flavor and other values by soaking in hot but not boiling water.
Stew	To boil or simmer in a small amount of liquid. Meats are stewed at simmering temperatures.
Toast	To brown, and occasionally blacken, by dry heat.

ONE INGREDIENT FOR ANOTHER

For these	Substitute these
1 whole egg, for thickening or baking	2 egg y o l k s. Or 1 tablespoon dried whole egg plus 2 tablespoons water. (Varies with product.)
1 whole egg in a batter	2 tablespoons of fresh dry snow, stirred in just before baking.
1 cup butter or margarine for shortening	$\frac{7}{8}$ cup of rendered bear or other animal fat, with $\frac{1}{2}$ teaspoon salt. Or 1 cup hydrogenated fat (cooking fat sold under brand name) with $\frac{1}{2}$ teaspoon salt.
1 square (ounce) chocolate	$3\frac{1}{2}$ tablespoons cocoa plus $\frac{1}{2}$ tablespoon fat.
Nut meats	Similar amount of browned rolled oats. Peanut butter will do, too.
1 teaspoon double acting baking powder	$1\frac{1}{2}$ teaspoons phosphate baking powder. Or 2 teaspoons tartrate baking powder.
Baking soda in breadstuffs	Equal amount of the white of hardwood ashes.
Sweet milk and baking powder, for baking	Equal amount of sour milk plus $\frac{1}{2}$ teaspoon soda per cup. (Each half teaspoon soda with 1 cup sour milk takes the place of 2 teaspoons baking powder and 1 cup sweet milk.)
1 cup sour milk, for baking	1 cup sweet milk mixed with one of the following: 1 tablespoon vinegar. Or 1 tablespoon lemon juice. Or $1\frac{3}{4}$ teaspoons cream of tartar.
1 cup whole milk	$\frac{1}{2}$ cup evaporated milk plus $\frac{1}{2}$ cup water. Or 4 tablespoons dry whole milk plus 1 cup water. (Varies.) Or $\frac{1}{3}$ cup nonfat dry milk plus $2\frac{1}{2}$ teaspoons

	table fat and ¾ cup water. (Varies.) Or 1 cup skim milk plus 2 tablespoons melted table fat or salad oil.
1 cup skim milk	⅓ cup nonfat dry milk plus ¾ cup water. (Varies.)
1 tablespoon flour, for thickening	½ tablespoon cornstarch, potato starch, rice starch, or arrowroot starch. Or 1 tablespoon granulated tapioca.
1 cup cake flour, for baking	⅞ cup all-purpose flour.
1 cup all-purpose flour, for baking breads	Up to ½ cup bran, whole-wheat flour, or corn meal plus enough all-purpose flour to fill cup.
Commercial jelling agent for jelly making	1 level teaspoon Epsom Salts for each 5 pounds of fruit.

MEASURING FOODS

Part of cup	A compact nest of aluminum measuring spoons will enable accuracy and can also be used for eating. Measure dry ingredients before liquids.
Cup	Check at home the relationship of nesting drinking cups to standard measuring cup. If necessary, mark.
Molasses, syrups	These will bother less with clinging and sticking if you'll either first chill the measuring implement in cold water or lightly grease it.
Sugar	Pack brown sugar firmly into cup or spoon. Press or sift any lumps out of granulated sugar and measure like flour.

Solid fats   When fat comes in one-pound rectangular form, 1 cup or fraction can be cut from pound which measures about 2 cups. With quarter-pound rectangles, each of these equals ½ cup or 8 tablespoons. You can measure a cupful, too, by packing firmly into cup and leveling off top with knife. Water method may be used for part of cup. To measure ½ cup fat, put ½ cup cold water in 1-cup measure. Add fat, pushing under water until water level stands at 1-cup mark. Pour out water and remove fat.

White flour   If you can, sift once onto a piece of plastic if that is most convenient. Lift lightly into cup. Don't pack. Don't shake or jar cup, or flour will settle down again. Level off top with knife.

Other flours   This also includes fine meals, fine crumbs, dried eggs, dry milks. Stir instead of sifting. Measure like flour.

Baking powder, etc.   Cornstarch, cream of tartar, and spices are included in this group. Stir to loosen. Fill spoon lightly to overflowing. Level with straight knife.

COMMON U. S. FOOD MEASURES

A dash, pinch, etc. . . . . less than ⅛ teaspoon
60 drops . . . . 1 teaspoon
3 teaspoons . . . . 1 tablespoon
2 tablespoons . . . . 1 fluid ounce
4 tablespoons . . . . ¼ cup

6 tablespoons .... ⅜ cup
8 tablespoons .... ½ cup
16 tablespoons .... 1 cup
1 cup .... 8 fluid ounces
2 cups .... 1 pint
1 gill .... ½ cup
4 gills .... 1 pint
1 pint .... 16 fluid ounces
2 pints .... 1 quart
1 quart .... 32 fluid ounces
4 quarts .... 1 gallon
1 pint milk or water .... 1 pound

CANADIAN LIQUID MEASURES

1 cup .... 8 fluid ounces
1 pint .... 20 fluid ounces
1 quart .... 40 fluid ounces
1 imperial quart .... 1¼ U. S. quarts
4 imperial quarts .... 1 imperial gallon
1 imperial gallon .... 5 U. S. quarts
One imperial quart, figured exactly, equals 1.2003 U. S. quarts.

DRY MEASURES

2 pints .... 1 quart
8 quarts .... 1 peck
4 pecks .... 1 bushel
British dry quart equals 1.0320 U. S. dry quarts.
Legal weights of a bushel of corn, barley, potatoes, etc. vary in different regions.

ORDINARY AVOIRDUPOIS WEIGHT

16 drams .... 1 ounce
16 ounces or 7000 grains .... 1 pound
14 pounds .... 1 stone
2000 pounds .... 1 short ton
2240 pounds .... 1 long ton

PROVISIONING TABLE

Calories	One-Pound Portion	Outfitting Data
2709	Almonds, shelled, dried	1 cup shelled—5⅓ oz.
1680	Apples, dried	1 lb. dried—8 lbs. fresh
1634	Apricots, dried	1 lb. dry—5½ lb. fresh
1047	Bacon, back	3 slices, 2½″ diam. x ¼″—3½ oz.
2855	Bacon, side	1 lb.—20 to 24 slices 2½ to 3 slices—2 oz.
1219	Banana, dried	3½ oz. dried—about 1 lb. fresh
1536	Barley, brown, whole	2 tbsp. dry—1 oz. yield ½ cup cooked
1525	Beans, dried, kidney	1 lb.—2⅔ cups 1 lb.—7 cups cooked
1512	Beans, Lima	1 lb.—2⅓ cups 1 lb.—6½ cups cooked
1535	Beans, Navy	1 lb.—2⅓ cups 1 lb.—6 cups cooked
977	Beef, corned, canned	3 slices 3″ x 2½″ x ¼″ —3½ oz.
922	Beef, dried or chipped	2 thin slices—1 oz.
1004	Bologna	1 slice—4½″ diam. x ⅛″—1 oz. 16 slices to 1 lb.
3248	Butter	1 lb.—2 cups
1587	Cabbage, dehydrated	1 lb. serves 50 1 serving ⅓ oz.
1641	Carrots, dehydrated	1 lb. serves 25 1 serving raw—4 oz. cooked
2619	Cashews	4 to 5 nuts—½ oz.
1804	Cheese, cheddar	1 lb. cheese grated— 4 cups
1676	Cheese, cheddar processed	

Calories	One-Pound Portion	Outfitting Data
433	Cheese, cottage	1 lb.—2 cups, serves 8
		1 serving, ¼ cup—2 oz.
1684	Cheese, cream	2 tablespoons—1 oz.
1679	Cheese, Swiss	1 slice, 4½″ x 3½″ x ⅛″—1 oz.
905	Chicken, canned, boned	½ cup—3½ oz.
2273	Chocolate, bitter	1 lb. melted—2 cups
2282	Chocolate, milk, plain	
2413	Chocolate, milk, with almonds	
2403	Chocolate, bittersweet	
2136	Chocolate, sweetened, plain	
1329	Cocoa, dry	1 lb.—4 cups
	Coffee, roasted	1 lb.—5½ cups finely ground, makes 50 cups. Contains, in solid state, 1316 calories.
1649	Corn meal, yellow	3 cups weigh 1 lb.
4013	Corn oil	1 lb.—2 cups
1642	Cornstarch	1 lb.—3½ cups (stirred)
4013	Cotton seed oil	1 lb.—2 cups
1287	Dates, dried, pitted	1 lb. pitted and cut—2½ cups
655	Eggs, fresh, whole	1 doz. extra large—27 oz. up
		1 doz. large—at least 24 oz.
		1 doz. medium—21 to 24 oz.
2688	Egg, dried, whole	¾ cup powder & 1½ cups water—1 doz. fresh eggs
1530	Farina, dark	3 tbsp. dry—1 oz. yield ¾ cup cooked

Calories	One-Pound Portion	Outfitting Data
1677	Farina, light	1 lb.—approximately 2⅔ cups dry
357	Figs, fresh, raw	2 medium—4 oz.
514	Figs, canned in syrup	½ cup weighs 3½ oz.
1223	Figs, dried	3 cups (44 figs)—1 lb.
2838	Filberts, shelled	1 cup—4¾ oz.
1643	Flour, buckwheat, light	1 cup—4¼ oz.
1574	Flour, dark	1 cup—4¼ oz.
1659	Flour, rye, light	1 lb. rye flour—about 4½ cups
		1 lb. sifted—5⅔ cups
1442	Flour, rye, dark	
1632	Flour, wheat	All-purpose flour—4 cups per lb. sifted
		Cake flour—4¾ cups per lb. sifted
		Pastry flour—4¾ cups per lb. sifted
1586	Flour, self-rising	4 cups per lb. sifted
1510	Flour, whole	Whole wheat flour stirred —3¾ cups per lb.
317	Fruit cocktail, canned	No. 2 can—1 lb.
1739	Gelatin, dessert powder	2½ cups per lb.
		1 oz. pkg. makes 4 to 6 servings
1643	Hominy, grits	3 cups per lb.
		3 tbsp. raw—⅔ cup cooked
1400	Honey	1 lb.—1⅓ cups
1262	Jam, assorted	3 level tbsp.—2 oz.
4091	Lard	2 cups per lb.
		1 oz. measures 2 tbsp.
1530	Lentils, dry	2⅓ cups per lb.
		2½ tbsp. dry—1 oz.— yields ½ cup cooked

Calories	One-Pound Portion	Outfitting Data
1928	Liverwurst	1 slice 3″ diameter ¼″ thick—1 oz.
1723	Macaroni	1 lb. 1″ pieces—4 cups 1 lb. cooked—12 cups—weighs 4 lbs.
624	Milk, evaporated	1 lb. tin & equal water—1½ pts. fresh milk
2231	Milk, powdered, whole	1 lb.—3½ cups 4 tbsp. level & 1 cup water—1 cup fresh milk
1642	Milk, powdered, skim	3.2 oz. makes 1 qt. ⅓ cup & ¾ cup water—1 cup fresh skim milk
1142	Molasses	1 cup weighs 11 oz.
107	Mushrooms, fresh, raw	4 large or 10 small—3½ oz.
1728	Noodles, containing egg	1″ pieces—6 cups to 1 lb. 1 lb. yields 11 cups cooked
1794	Oats, meal or rolled	1 lb.—5⅔ cups ⅓ cup makes 1 cup porridge
3266	Oleomargarine	1 tbsp.—½ oz.
4013	Olive oil	1 lb.—2 cups
308	Peaches, canned in syrup	2 halves & 3 tbsp. juice—4 oz.
1634	Peaches, dried	1 lb. dried—5½ lbs. fresh
2613	Peanut butter	1 lb.—2 cups
1219	Pears, dried	1 lb. dried—5½ lbs. fresh
193	Peas, fresh	2.2 lbs. whole—1 lb. shelled (3 cups)
1540	Peas, dried, green	2 tbsp. dry—1 oz. yields ½ cup cooked

Calories	One-Pound Portion	Outfitting Data
1562	Peas, split	2¼ cups—1 lb.
3159	Pecans, shelled	1 lb. in shell yields ⅓ lb. meats
3410	Pork, salt, fat, with rind	2 slices 4″ x 2″ x ⅜″— 3½ oz.
318	Potatoes, fresh	1 lb. as purchased—3 to 4 servings
1620	Potatoes, dehydrated	1 serving—1 oz. dry—4 oz. reconstituted
1034	Prunes, dried, with pits	Sizes—large 20 to 40 per lb., medium 40 to 60 per pound., small 60 to 100 per lb.
1725	Prunes, dried, pitted	1 lb. cooked with 2 qts. water gives 2½ qts.
1217	Raisins, dried	Seeded, 3¼ cups—1 lb. Seedless, whole, 2¾ cups —1 lb.
1648	Rice, brown	2 tbsp. dry—1 oz. yields ½ cup cooked
1629	Rice, white	1 lb.—2⅛ cups, 7 cups when cooked
1682	Rice, wild	1 lb.—3 cups 1 oz.—3 tbsp.—1 serving
1787	Salad dressing, French	2 tbsp.—1 oz.
3211	Salad dressing, mayonnaise	2 tbsp.—1 oz.
1531	Sardines in oil	15 sardines 3″ long— 5 oz.
784	Sardines in tomato sauce	
1817	Sausage, salami in casing	1 slice 4½″ diam., ⅛″ thick—1 oz.
1164	Sausage, weiners, raw	7 to 9 per lb.
4010	Shortening, vegetable, Crisco, Spry, etc.	1 lb.—2¼ cups

Calories	One-Pound Portion	Outfitting Data
1719	Spaghetti	1 lb. broken—4¾ cups
3437	Suet	1 lb. ground suet—3½ cups
1676	Sugar, brown	2 cups (firmly packed)—1 lb.
1747	Sugar, granulated, white	1 lb.—2¼ cups
1747	Sugar, icing	1 lb.—3½ cups
1747	Sugar, loaf	Flat tablets, 100 to 1 lb.
1580	Sugar, maple	1 piece 1″ x 1¼″ x ½″—½ oz.
1299	Syrups, corn	1⅓ cups per lb.
1123	Syrups, maple	1½ cups per lb.
1633	Tapioca, dry, pearl	2¾ cups raw—7½ cups cooked
	Tea	1 lb.—6 cups dry makes 200 to 300 cups
2969	Walnuts, shelled	1 lb. in shell—½ lb. meats
		1 lb. halves—4½ cups
1639	Wheat, germ	1 tbsp.—1/6 oz.
1544	Whole wheat, dry	⅓ cup dry—1 oz.—¾ cup cooked

This chart may be used for scientifically planning a light and compact grubstake made up largely of high-energy rations.

The nutrient values, based on official researches of two governments with standard United States and Canadian foods, will vary somewhat in different localities. Dehydrated products will, naturally, differ to an even broader extent, depending not only on the original raw products but also on processing methods. Seasonal variations have not been noted, being minor in the aspects here considered.

WILDERNESS COOKERY

Outdoor trips have a way of sneaking up on an individual. Better start planning now for that next adventure back of beyond.

You're not going vacationing to spend your time cooking and eating. On the other hand, the right kind of meals will never taste better than when appetites are sharpened to a wonderful edge by healthful outdoor living.

EXTRA RECIPES

EXTRA RECIPES

NEXT TIME BRING:

INDEX